EFFECTIVE EXECUTIVE'S

The Seven Core Skills Required to Turn Office into a Business Power Tool

GUIDE TO OFFICE XP

D1315059

EFFECTIVE EXECUTIVE'S

The Seven Core Skills Required to Turn Office into a Business Power Tool

GUIDE TO OFFICE XP

Carolyn M. Connally
Stephen L. Nelson

REDMOND
TECHNOLOGY
PRESS

Effective Executive's Guide to Office XP:
The Seven Core Skills Required to Turn Office into a Business Power Tool
Copyright © 2001 Stephen L. Nelson & Carolyn M. Connally

Published by
Redmond Technology Press
8581 154th Avenue NE
Redmond, WA 98052
www.redtechpress.com

Library of Congress Catalog Card No: applied for

ISBN 1-931150-07-9

Printed and bound in the United States of America.

9 8 7 6 5 4 3 2 1

Distributed by
Independent Publishers Group
814 N. Franklin St.
Chicago, IL 60610
www.ipgbook.com

Product and company names mentioned herein may be the trademarks of their respective owners.

In the preparation of this book, both the author and the publisher have made every effort to provide current, correct, and comprehensible information. Nevertheless, inadvertent errors can occur and software and the principles and regulations concerning business often change. Furthermore, the application and impact of principles, rules, and laws can vary widely from case to case because of the unique facts involved. For these reasons, the author and publisher specifically disclaim any liability or loss that is incurred as a consequence of the use and application, directly or indirectly, of any information presented in this book. If legal or other expert assistance is needed, the services of a professional should be sought.

Dedication

I dedicate this book to those for whom Office skills are strange and intimidating. It is my sincere hope that this book helps to bring light out of the darkness. CMC

Acknowledgments

I wish to acknowledge the support of those family members and friends who believed in me and supported me through the writing of this book, as well as those at Redmond Technology Press, whose patience was unbounded. CMC

Contents at a Glance

Contents

Skill 3 **Use Outlook for Easy Organization**   **47**

Skill 4   **Use Word for Document Generation**   **75**

Skill 6   Use PowerPoint for Powerful Presentations   133

Skill 7 **Use Access for Data Management** 171

Appendix A **Use Object Linking and Embedding** 199

INTRODUCTION

When Microsoft first offered its leading business software programs packaged as a suite product, it was a brilliant marketing mechanism. Not only was it a convenient purchase for the end user but the interaction between the products was revolutionary. The product suite became a standard across the entire software industry.

The newest Microsoft Office version is a proud progeny of the first Office suite. More powerful and more convenient than ever before, its component programs are cutting edge.

We've written *Effective Executive's Guide to Office* to get you started using the essential Office applications; or, if you are already an office user, to guide you through the techniques where they might be different from earlier versions. Our intent is not to make you a Power User, but to make you comfortable enough with the applications that you can use them right away and know enough to gradually explore the multitude of uses not discussed in this book.

What This Book Assumes About You

This book assumes that you are already familiar with the Microsoft Windows environment. You are not going to find detailed information here about using menus, dialog boxes, and such. If you do not already know how to work with these Windows essentials, then we suggest that you learn these techniques before proceeding with this book. You can acquire the needed skills through the Microsoft Web site, a quick lesson from a friend, or a good introductory book.

How This Book Is Organized

We have broken Microsoft Office into seven basic skills. Each of the five applications in this book, Outlook, Word, Excel, PowerPoint, and Access, are discussed as one of the seven skills. In addition, the book begins with two chapters on skills that are common to all Office applications. The seven skills, or chapters, are described below.

Skill 1: Use Common Office Tools

One of the great advantages of the Office suite of programs is that the applications look, and to a certain extent, act alike. There is great similarity between the Standard and Formatting toolbars, for example. These common tools are discussed in Skill 1 where you learn about toolbars, the Clipboard, and Office Help.

Skill 2: Manage Files

In the Office environment, file management is consistent from one program to another. Therefore, we have grouped file management techniques into Skill 2. Here you learn to create a new file, save it, close it, and open it again. You also learn how to print from any of the applications.

Skill 3: Use Outlook for Easy Organization

Outlook is a great workhorse of an application. You can use it to send and receive your e-mail, keep track of your appointments and contacts, and manage your tasks. Each of these functions of Outlook is discussed in Skill 3.

Skill 4: Use Word for Document Generation

Word processing is the single most important skill needed in business today. Everyone needs to know how to create and edit documents. And that is what is included in Skill 4, plus some handy timesaving features.

Skill 5: Use Excel for Spreadsheet Functions

All of the basic functions of Excel are discussed in this chapter. From writing formulas and using functions to formatting data and creating charts—everything you need to know is discussed in Skill 5.

Skill 6: Use PowerPoint for Powerful Presentations

For information on creating professional presentations, turn to Skill 6. This chapter takes you from creating a basic presentation to applying design templates and adding PowerPoint animation for a knock-your-socks-off effect. We've even included some guidelines for effective presentations.

Skill 7: Use Access for Data Management

Access is a powerful and sophisticated relational database program. If you are an experienced database user, moving to Access from another program is easy with the information contained in Skill 7. If you are new to the world of databases, the discussions here on the four basic elements of Access get you started.

NOTE   *In addition to the seven skills, Appendix A contains information on Object Linking and Embedding, a particularly valuable tool for business. The book also includes a glossary and an index.*

Conventions Used in This Book

This book is intended to take the form of a casual conversation such as you might have with a coworker. We want the atmosphere of this book to be what you would find in a one-on-one discussion or a small group workshop. The use of the pronoun *we* refers to the two authors, not an imperial or editorial affectation.

Another convention concerns references to buttons, boxes, and menu items. To set these items off from the regular text, we capitalize initial letters of the words that comprise their labels. So, while the labels may not show capitalization of all the initial letters, we are doing so to identify the reference as a label.

Skill 1

USE COMMON OFFICE TOOLS

Featuring:

- The Office Assistant
- Office Help Without the Office Assistant
- Reviewing the Office Toolbars
- The Office Shortcut Bar
- The Clipboard

The Microsoft Office programs use a common set of features and tools. Before you begin working with the individual applications, therefore, you'll want to familiarize yourself with these tools. You'll see them in most or all of the applications.

The Office Assistant

One of the first things you notice when you begin using Office is a cartoon character, called an Office Assistant. When you have a question, the Office Assistant helps you find the answer.

Using the Office Assistant

Clicking the Office Assistant image brings up a list of topics that you access by clicking one of the topics. These topics are context sensitive; in other words, they are based upon the context of your application usage at that time.

If none of these topics meets your needs, enter your question in the box provided and click Search, as shown in Figure 1-1. The Office Assistant then displays a list of topics that correspond to your question. Clicking any one of those topics opens the contents in a window to the right of your screen.

Figure 1-1   Asking a question of the Office Assistant.

TIP   *Another way to get help from the Office Assistant is by typing a question in the box on the menu bar where it says "Type a question for help."*

Customizing the Office Assistant

You can change the character used for the Office Assistant by choosing from the several assistants that are available. To select a different character, right-click the Office Assistant image and choose Choose Assistant from the shortcut menu. Use the Next or Back buttons to scroll through the various characters, as shown in Figure 1-2. Make your choice by clicking OK.

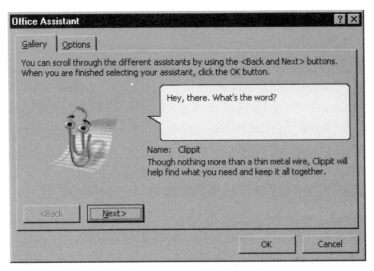

Figure 1-2   The Office Assistant dialog box.

Further customization of the Office Assistant is available through the same process. On the Options tab, you can make any of several changes to the operation of the Office Assistant by selecting or clearing the check boxes, as shown in Figure 1-3.

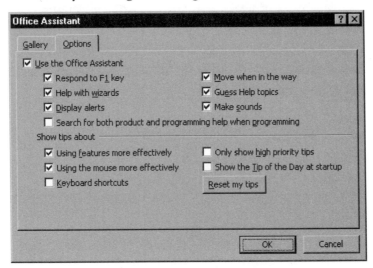

Figure 1-3   The Office Assistant dialog box open at the Options tab.

Right-clicking the Office Assistant also allows you to hide the Assistant so that, while still active, it no longer appears on your screen. When hidden, the Office Assistant automatically reappears when the program determines that you need assistance. Clicking the Help button (with a question mark on it) on the Standard toolbar also causes the Office Assistant to reappear.

Deactivating the Office Assistant

Once you are more familiar with the Office applications, you may find that amusement with the Office Assistant has worn thin. Fortunately, removing the Assistant is an easy process. Right-click the Office Assistant image, choose Options from the shortcut menu, and then clear the Use The Office Assistant check box. The Office Assistant is now no longer displayed. You can redisplay the Office Assistant by choosing the Help menu's Show The Office Assistant command.

Office Help Without the Office Assistant

Although the Office Assistant is an integral part of the Office Help system, the Help system without the Assistant is a powerful database of information that goes far beyond any previous Help systems in providing you with the answers you need. Understanding the ways in which you can utilize Office Help is an important part of learning to use Office effectively.

Choose the Help menu's Microsoft Word Help command to open the Help dialog box, as shown in Figure 1-4. If the Contents, Answer Wizard, and Index tabs aren't visible, click the Show button. Then click Contents, Answer Wizard, or Index to conduct your help search.

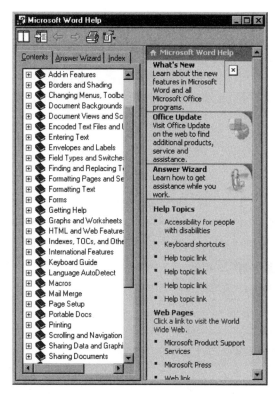

Figure 1-4   The Help dialog box in Word.

Using Help Contents

The Help Contents tab is arranged just like the table of contents in a book. Main categories of information are called chapters. Topic categories are listed under chapters with subtopics under them.

To find a discussion that gives you the information you need, follow these steps:

1. Locate a chapter.

Scroll through the chapter headings indicated by the book-shaped icons, and click the one that seems to contain your topic. Chapter and subchapter icons are shaped as closed books. A question-mark icon indicates a topic page.

2. Expand the chapter.

Clicking the plus sign to the left of a chapter icon expands the chapter so that you can see the subchapters or topics contained in it. When a chapter is expanded, its icon resembles an open book. Clicking a minus sign to the left of a chapter icon collapses the chapter, hiding all subchapters and returning the icon to a closed book.

3. Expand a subchapter.

Continue to expand subchapters until you locate the topic that contains the discussion you need.

4. Select a topic.

Click the topic that meets your needs. The topic pages appear in the window to the right side of the Help dialog box, as shown in Figure 1-5.

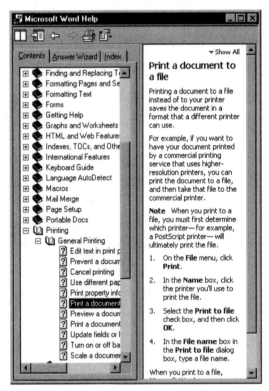

Figure 1-5   The Help Contents tab.

Using the Answer Wizard

The Answer Wizard allows you to use Office's natural language interface for locating help topics. To use this Help feature, follow these steps:

1. Open the Answer Wizard.

Click the Answer Wizard tab. The Answer Wizard opens and asks "What would you like to do?"

2. Ask the Answer Wizard a question.

Enter a question in the space provided. Click Search. A list of help topics appears in the Select Topic To Display list.

3. Select a topic.

Click the appropriate topic to reveal its discussion in the window on the right side of the Help dialog box, as shown in Figure 1-6.

Figure 1-6   The Help Answer Wizard tab.

Using the Help Index

Use the Help Index just as you would the index of a book by looking up your topic alphabetically. To do this, follow these steps:

1. Type a topic word.

Enter the first few letters of a topic in the Type Keywords box, as shown in Figure 1-7. As you type, the Help system locates your topic.

2. Select a keyword.

When the keyword appears that most closely matches the information you need, double-click that keyword. Topic titles appear in the box below.

3. Select a topic title.

Look through the topic titles in the box below the Keyword box. The topic page appears on the right pane of the Help window.

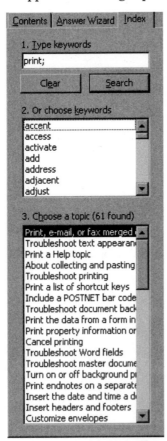

Figure 1-7   The Help Index tab.

Help Options

Once you locate the information you need, you can use the Help dialog box as you work in your application by leaving it on the screen or you can print it. The printer icon on the Help toolbar displays your Print dialog box so that you can send the topic page to the printer.

Also on the Help toolbar is a Show/Hide button that displays or hides the tab section of the dialog box. Back and Forward buttons let you review topics you have been working with and then return to your original place.

Help on the Web

Choosing the Help menu's Office On The Web command automatically connects you to the Office Update site on the Internet. This site positions you to use the power of the Internet to find more valuable Office information.

NOTE *To be automatically connected to the Office Update site, you must have an open Internet connection. If you use a dial-up connection, start it prior to choosing Office On The Web.*

Reviewing the Office Toolbars

Toolbar buttons and boxes provide shortcuts to common tasks or commands. Each program contains multiple toolbars for use with the different functions of that application.

The common toolbar that appears in all five of the Office applications is the Standard toolbar. The Standard toolbar holds the buttons most used in operation of the application, as shown in Figure 1-8. For example, the buttons for New, Open, Save, and Print are available on the Standard toolbar in Word, Excel, PowerPoint, and Access. In Outlook, the Standard toolbar changes with each of the Outlook functions (Inbox, Calendar, Contacts, and Tasks). Each version of the Standard toolbar contains a New button and a Print button as well as buttons appropriate to the application.

Figure 1-8   The Standard toolbar in Word.

Another common toolbar found in four of the five applications (Outlook being the exception) is the Formatting toolbar, as shown in Figure 1-9. As its name reflects, this toolbar contains buttons and boxes that provide formatting options for the file created using the application. The Formatting toolbar appears by default in Word, Excel, and PowerPoint. It is available in Access when using those functions that require its use.

Figure 1-9   The Formatting toolbar in Excel.

Also found in Word, Excel, and PowerPoint is the Drawing toolbar, which can be used to create and format graphics within the application. This toolbar appears identically within each of the three programs, as shown in Figure 1-10.

Figure 1-10   The Drawing toolbar in PowerPoint.

The number of toolbars differs from one application to the next (from 29 in Word to four in Outlook). To display a particular toolbar, right-click any toolbar to reveal the Toolbars shortcut menu, as shown in Figure 1-11. Select the check box for the toolbar you want to display from the list shown. To hide a toolbar, right-click any toolbar to reveal the shortcut menu and then clear the check box for the toolbar you want to close by clicking it.

Figure 1-11   The Toolbars shortcut menu.

Although the most commonly used toolbars are shown on the shortcut menu, there may be additional toolbars available in the program. To locate additional toolbars, right-click any toolbar and choose Customize from the shortcut menu. The Customize dialog box opens at the Toolbars tab, as shown in Figure 1-12. This dialog box lists all toolbars. Select toolbars by clicking the appropriate boxes to check or clear them.

Figure 1-12 The Customize dialog box open at the Toolbars tab.

In Access, the toolbars available to you change depending upon which window you are working in. For example, when the Database window is open you have the choice of the Standard (Database) toolbar and the Web toolbar; but in a Table window, you have a list that contains the Clipboard, Formatting, Standard (Table Datasheet), and Web toolbars.

In Office, the Standard and Formatting toolbars appear on one line by default so that less screen space is used. Only the most frequently used buttons of the toolbars show. More toolbar buttons can be displayed by using your mouse to drag the overlapping toolbar left or right as needed to see all buttons. The toolbars can be rearranged by clicking the small arrow at the end of the toolbar. Select Show Buttons On Two Rows from the drop-down menu and the Formatting toolbar appears below the Standard toolbar.

Customizing Toolbars

Within all of the Office applications, you can customize any existing toolbars or even create a new toolbar with the buttons you use most. Toolbars can be moved to new locations on your computer screen.

Adding Tools to Toolbars

In Office, adding or removing commonly used commands is easy. Just click the small arrow at the end of the toolbar, select Add Or Remove Buttons from the drop-down menu, and select buttons from the list provided.

To add commands that are not reflected in the list, follow these steps:

1. Open the Commands tab of the Customize dialog box.

Right-click a toolbar, and choose Customize from the shortcut menu. When the Customize dialog box appears, click the Commands tab, as shown in Figure 1-13.

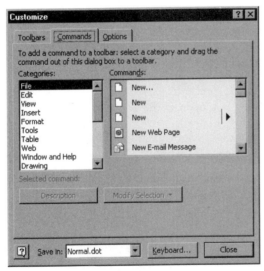

Figure 1-13 The Customize dialog box open at the Commands tab.

2. Select the category of commands that you want.

Scroll through the Categories list on the left for the category most likely to provide the command you want to add to the toolbar. Click the category of your choice.

3. **Select the specific command you want to add to the toolbar.**

After you select a category, all the commands available within it show in the Commands list on the right. Scroll through the commands, and select the one you want to add to a toolbar. If you are unsure of any of the command functions, select a command and click the Description button. A short description of the selected command appears on your screen.

4. **Drag the command to a convenient location on the toolbar.**

When you locate the command you want, click it and drag it to the toolbar. Release the mouse button to drop the new command where you want it.

NOTE   *While the Customize dialog box is open, you can also drag buttons from the toolbar into the document area of your screen to remove them.*

5. **After all changes have been made, close the Customize dialog box.**

Make all the changes you want to make, and then click the Close button to close the dialog box.

Moving Toolbars

The layout of toolbars on your screen is established by default in an arrangement considered to be convenient for most users. For example, the Standard and Formatting toolbars are located at the top of the application window; the Drawing toolbar is located at the bottom. However, you can change the location of any toolbar merely by dragging it to a new position. Toolbars dragged to any of the four sides of the screen are locked into position but can be moved by dragging on any of the lines in the toolbar. Move toolbars that float on your screen by dragging the top border (for example, the title bar).

Creating a New Toolbar

To create a new toolbar with the buttons you use most often, follow these steps:

1. **Open the Toolbars tab of the Customize dialog box.**

Right-click any toolbar, and then choose Customize from the shortcut menu. When the Customize dialog box opens, the Toolbars tab may be the active tab. If you have recently used another tab, however, you may need to click the Toolbars tab to select it.

2. Create a new toolbar.

Click New to open the New Toolbar dialog box, as shown in Figure 1-14. Type a name for the new toolbar in the Toolbar Name box. When you click OK, a new toolbar appears on your screen; however, it is very small because it has no buttons.

Figure 1-14 The New Toolbar dialog box in Excel.

NOTE   *Word has a second box in the New Toolbar dialog box. The Make Toolbar Available To box shows Normal.dot by default. In most cases, you should leave this as it is. Normal.dot (the Normal template) makes the toolbar available to all new Word documents you create.*

3. Add commands to your new toolbar.

To add commands to your toolbar, first click the Commands tab. Add buttons by locating the commands you want and dragging them to your toolbar. The toolbar enlarges to accommodate all the buttons. If you add more buttons than will fit on a single line on your screen, the toolbar wraps to a second line. Treat your customized toolbar as any other Office toolbar.

To delete a customized toolbar, open the Customize dialog box to the Toolbars tab. Select the toolbar you want to delete, and click Delete. The toolbar is permanently deleted.

NOTE   *You should delete only those toolbars you have created. If you delete a toolbar that is innate with the application, it can be recovered only by reinstalling the Office application on your computer.*

The Office Shortcut Bar

As soon as Office is installed on your computer, you may notice a group of buttons within the title bar of each application window, as shown in Figure 1-15. This is the Office shortcut bar. The shortcut bar provides rapid, one-click access to the Office applications or to any program or document on your computer.

Figure 1-15 The Office shortcut bar.

NOTE *The Office shortcut bar may appear along the right side of your screen instead of on the title bar. The bar works the same in either location, and you can move it where you prefer it.*

Using the Office Shortcut Bar

The shortcut bar contains buttons that connect you to items such as Create A New Office Document, New Appointment, New Message, and Screen Saver, as well as the Office applications. Buttons that provide access to other Office functions are easily activated. Additionally, the shortcut bar can be customized to include buttons that start other applications or open frequently accessed documents. Other essential toolbars, such as Desktop, Favorites, and Accessories, can be made a part of the shortcut bar as well.

Adding Buttons to Your Shortcut Bar

To add frequently used buttons to your shortcut bar, follow these steps:

1. **Open the View tab of the Customize dialog box.**

   Right-click the Office shortcut bar just to the right of the logo but to the left of the first button, and choose Customize from the shortcut menu. The Customize dialog box usually opens with the View tab displayed. If not, click the View tab to make it the active page.

2. **Select the toolbar you want to edit.**

   If you have selected more than one toolbar to be available on your Office shortcut bar (see the section "Adding Toolbars to Your Shortcut Bar," below), you must select the toolbar you want to change. Click the drop-down arrow to open the Toolbar list box, and select the toolbar you want to edit.

3. **Click the Buttons tab, and choose buttons.**

   Click the Buttons tab to open it. All the buttons displayed on your Office shortcut bar are shown with check marks beside them. Other buttons may also be available. Customize the shortcut bar toolbar by selecting check boxes or clearing them, as shown in Figure 1-16.

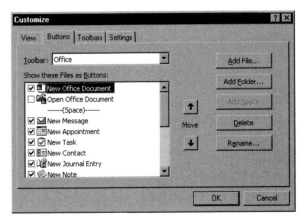

Figure 1-16 The Customize dialog box open at the Buttons tab.

NOTE *Selecting an item and clicking the Delete button may permanently remove that item from its original location as well. For example, if you have a document on your Office toolbar, deleting it from the toolbar removes it from your computer.*

Adding a Folder, a Program, or a Document to Your Shortcut Bar

You can add buttons to your shortcut bar that provide instant access to any folder, program, or document on your computer. Just follow these steps:

1. **Open the View tab of the Customize dialog box.**

   Open the Customize dialog box by right-clicking the Office shortcut bar to the right of the logo but to the left of the first button and choosing Customize from the shortcut menu. The Customize dialog box usually opens with the View tab displayed. If it does not, click the View tab.

2. **Select the toolbar you want to edit.**

   If you have selected more than one toolbar to be available on your Office shortcut bar (see the section "Adding Toolbars to Your Shortcut Bar," below), you must select the toolbar to which you want to add buttons. Click the drop-down arrow to open the Toolbar list box, and select the toolbar to which you want to add buttons, as shown in Figure 1-17.

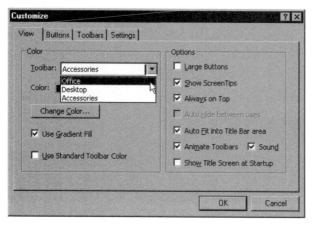

Figure 1-17 Selecting a toolbar from the Customize dialog box.

3. Open the Buttons tab.

Click the Buttons tab. All the buttons currently available to that toolbar are listed on this tab. The ones currently displayed on the toolbar have a check mark beside them. Others that are available but not in use are not marked.

4. Click the Add File or the Add Folder button.

Use the Add File button to insert a program or document. The Add Folder button provides access to a folder from which you select a program, document, or function. Click the appropriate button. A new dialog box opens that allows you to locate the file or folder of your choice.

5. Browse to locate and select the file or folder you want to add to your toolbar.

From the Add File or the Add Folder dialog box, locate the item you want to add to the shortcut bar. Use the Look In drop-down list box, as shown in Figure 1-18, to locate the item by finding and opening its parent folder. Folders can be identified by the folder icon to the left of their name. If you want to add an application, you must locate the .exe file for that application. A document is identified by its name. Once located, click the file or folder, and click the Add button.

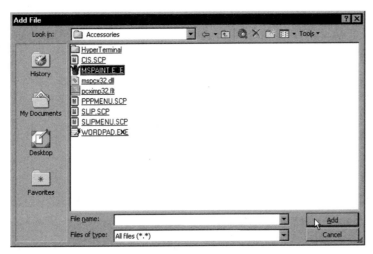

Figure 1-18 Selecting an item from the Add File dialog box.

6. Close the Customize dialog box.

Click OK when you are finished to save your changes and close the dialog box.

Adding Toolbars to Your Shortcut Bar

When you access the shortcut bar menu (by right-clicking the shortcut bar to the right of the logo and to the left of the first button), notice the list of possible toolbars that appears. By default, only the Office toolbar is selected. Any of the following five toolbars may be selected as well:

- Desktop—This shortcut bar toolbar displays every item that you have stored on your desktop. Having this shortcut bar handy provides easy access to desktop icons such as My Computer or Internet Explorer when they are covered up by other windows.

- Quick Shelf—By default, the Quick Shelf toolbar is empty. It provides you a place where you can keep your frequently used documents, programs, and folders within one-click accessibility.

- Favorites—The Favorites shortcut bar displays every one of the sites you have saved on your Internet Explorer Favorites list. Clicking any of the Favorites opens the Internet Explorer browser and takes you to that site.

- Programs—All the applications listed on your Programs list from the Start menu are displayed on this shortcut bar toolbar.

- Accessories—This toolbar displays accessories such as Paint, Games, or System Tools.

Selecting the check box next to a toolbar name places it on the Shortcut bar, allowing you to toggle between the Office toolbar and the new toolbar.

NOTE   *Keep in mind that if you select the Favorites toolbar, for example, every one of your Internet favorites appears on the toolbar. For many, this would be more buttons than could be shown in the space available. Click to clear most of the buttons as described above, leaving checked only those to which you need easy access.*

The Clipboard

The Clipboard is a feature of Office that allows you to reposition or replicate objects with ease. The Clipboard holds as many as 24 objects that you have cut or copied and enables you to paste them into a new location or multiple locations as you wish.

Clipboard Terminology

As you begin working with the Clipboard, it is useful to understand several key terms:

- Object—An object is any graphic, text, spreadsheet cell or range of cells, or other document element that can be selected by the mouse.

- Cut—Cutting an object means that you are removing the object from its location and placing it on the Clipboard so that it can be pasted elsewhere. If you want to move an object, this is the command you use.

- Copy—Copying an object means that you leave it where it is in a document while placing a copy of it on the Clipboard so that you can paste it into additional locations.

- Paste—Pasting an object places the object at a desired location within a document.

- Clipboard pane—The Clipboard pane contains the last 24 objects that have been cut or copied onto the Clipboard. Access it by choosing the Edit menu's Office Clipboard command.

NOTE   *A keyboard shortcut to open the Clipboard pane is to press Ctrl+C, twice. Note that if any text is selected it will be copied into the Clipboard.*

Cutting or Copying an Object

To cut or copy an object, you must first select it by clicking it. In the case of text or spreadsheet cells, click where you want the object to begin and drag your mouse through the text or cells to the end. Once the object has been selected, choose either the Cut (to move) or the Copy (to replicate) command from the Edit menu. Cut and Copy buttons are on the Standard toolbar, as well, for convenience, as shown in Figure 1-19.

Figure 1-19   The Cut, Copy, and Paste buttons from the Formatting toolbar.

Pasting an Object

Once you have placed an object on the Clipboard, it remains there unless it is replaced by another object, you delete it, or you close Office. When 24 items have been cut or copied onto the Clipboard, the 25th object replaces the first, and so forth. As long as an object remains in the Clipboard, you can paste it into as many locations as you want.

To paste the last object cut or copied onto the Clipboard, place your insertion point where you want the object to be located and choose the Edit menu's Paste command or click the Paste button on the Standard toolbar.

To paste a previously cut or copied object, first position your insertion point where you want the object to be placed and then choose the File menu's Office Clipboard command. The program displays a list of the objects on the Clipboard in a separate pane to the right side of your screen, as shown in Figure 1-20. Clicking the object of your choice pastes it into your document.

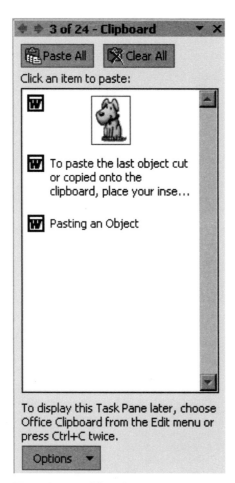

Figure 1-20 The Clipboard pane.

MANAGE FILES

Featuring:

- Creating a New File
- Saving a File
- Closing a File
- Opening an Existing File
- Printing a File

Although the Microsoft Office programs differ greatly in purpose and the data they utilize, all of the programs manage documents in a very similar manner. In this skill, we discuss how to create, save, close, open, and print your files effectively.

NOTE *The processed and formatted information generated by any Office program may be called a* file *or a* document. *You can consider the two terms to be synonymous.*

Creating a New File

Although Office files differ greatly from one program to another, no matter which program you use, you create a file using one of two techniques:

- Use the Standard toolbar.
- Use the File menu's New command.

NOTE   *If you are currently working within a file in Word, Excel, PowerPoint, or Access, creating a new document opens the new one in addition to the one you are currently using. You can switch back and forth between the two (or more) by using the taskbar buttons or the Windows menu.*

Creating a New File from the Standard Toolbar

On the Standard toolbar of Word, Excel, PowerPoint, and Access, the first button is the New button. It contains an icon that resembles a clean piece of paper, as shown in Figure 2-1.

Figure 2-1   The New button on Word's Standard toolbar.

Clicking the New button produces a new document in Word (based on your usual settings) or a new workbook in Excel ready for data entry. In PowerPoint, clicking the New button creates a new presentation and displays the Slide Layout pane, as shown in Figure 2-2, from which you can choose the layout of the first file in the presentation.

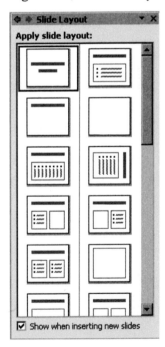

Figure 2-2   The Slide Layout pane in PowerPoint.

In Access, however, clicking the New button displays the New pane identical to that which is discussed later in this skill in the section "Creating a New Document from the File Menu."

In Outlook, the New button is also present on the Standard toolbar, but the item created by the New button in Outlook differs from one Outlook function to another. If you are working in Calendar, the New button opens a dialog box in which you can enter the details of a new appointment. In the Inbox function, you get an Untitled Message form with which you could send an e-mail message. In the Contacts function, clicking the New button displays a New Contact form, as shown in Figure 2-3, and so forth.

Figure 2-3   The New Contacts button in Outlook.

Additionally, the New button in Outlook contains a drop-down arrow. Clicking this arrow displays a list from which you can select the new item from any of Outlook's functions. In other words, you can choose to send a new e-mail message while you are working with the Calendar function.

Creating a New Document from the File Menu

Using menu commands instead of toolbar buttons takes one or two more mouse clicks but usually gives you more choices in the setup of the function you are using. The File menu's New command is no exception. In Word, Excel, PowerPoint, and Access, choosing the File menu's New command displays a New pane from which you can choose the type of file you want to create (or open). Figure 2-4 shows the New Document pane as it appears in Word.

Figure 2-4   The New Document pane in Word.

The New pane is divided into four main categories, which describe almost any type of file creation or retrieval that you may want.

Open Section

The Open section of the New pane retrieves previously created files. We discuss this later in this skill in the section "Opening an Existing File."

New Section

The New section of the pane enables the creation of a new file. Blank Document [Workbook, Presentation, Database] opens a new, blank document, based on your usual settings for that program. Other choices may be offered, such as Blank Web Page and Blank E-Mail Message in Word or Blank Data Access Page in Access.

New From Existing Section

If you want to create a new document that is very similar to one already saved in your system, the New From Existing section makes it easy to open a copy of that file. Click the Choose Document [Workbook, Presentation, File] option, and locate the file you want to duplicate. When you select the document and click OK, it is copied and displayed as an unnamed document.

New From Template Section

When creating a document with formatting different from what you usually use, you may want to use a template (a type of document with usage-specific formatting). Each program displays a General Templates option on the New pane as well as Templates On My Web Sites and Templates On Microsoft.com. General Templates opens a dialog box with a list of templates available in that program categorized on multiple tabs, as shown in Figure 2-5. In some cases, selecting a template reveals a preview on the right side of the dialog box. After selecting the template you want, clicking OK opens the template as an unnamed document preformatted to specific parameters.

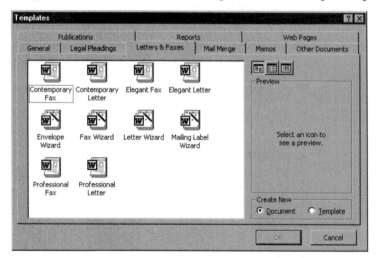

Figure 2-5   The Templates dialog box in Word.

For example, in Word you might choose a Professional Fax template. The document would open formatted as a Fax transmittal, as shown in Figure 2-6. All you would need to do is enter the specific information.

Figure 2-6 The Professional Fax template in Word.

In Excel, if you chose the Time Card template, the workbook would open preformatted as a timecard, as shown in Figure 2-7. All you would need to do is enter your company information and the relevant data.

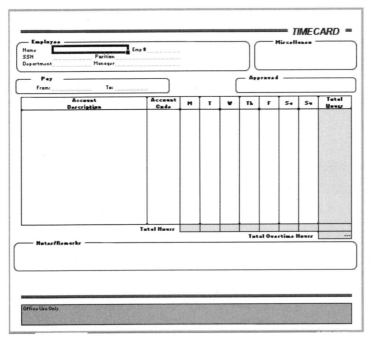

Figure 2-7 The Timecard template in Excel.

The Template dialog box also offers you the opportunity of using a wizard. A wizard is an easy-to-use mini program, within an Office program, that automatically creates and formats a particular type of file. When you select a wizard icon from the Template dialog box and click OK, the wizard asks you questions as to your preferences of content and layout, as shown in Figure 2-8. When you have finished running the wizard, your project is essentially completed; you only need to enter the body text of the document or modify the text created by the wizard. As you become more familiar with the Office programs, try using the wizards; they can be great time-savers.

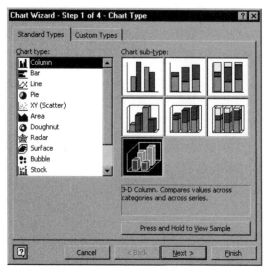

Figure 2-8   The Chart Wizard in Excel.

In Outlook, choosing the File menu's New command opens a submenu from which you can choose any Outlook item.

Saving a File

As anyone who has used computers for any length of time knows all too well, saving your file on a regular basis is essential. While you are working on your file, the data is held in a temporary storage area called memory. Your data is not permanently stored on your hard drive (or other storage medium) until you have chosen the Save command. If you experience a power outage or a computer problem requiring a restart, your memory is cleared of data. Any information that you have entered, and not yet saved, may be lost. It is a good idea to develop a habit of saving your files every few minutes.

NOTE   *Office programs provide a feature called AutoRecover that lets you tell the Office program to regularly save your file to disk. We talk about this helpful feature later in this skill.*

To Save or Save As

The Save As command allows you to name your file and specify where it is to be saved; the Save command is used to save changes to a document that has already been named.

If you have not yet named your document and click the Save button on the toolbar or choose the File menu's Save command, the Save As dialog box appears. That means that you don't have to be concerned as to which command to select, the Office program takes you to the right spot.

If you want to create a second document identical to the one you are working on, but with a different name, use the Save As command.

The Save As Dialog Box

The Save As dialog box is used to name your file and to select a location in which to save it. Just follow these steps:

1. Open the Save As dialog box.

Choose the File menu's Save As command and the Save As dialog box opens, as shown in Figure 2-9. However, if your document is not named, the File menu's Save command produces the same result.

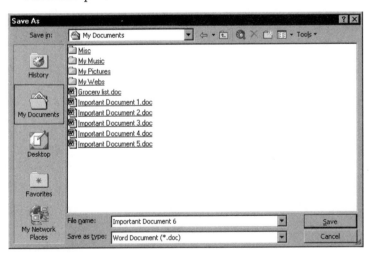

Figure 2-9   The Save As dialog box.

2. **Identify a location for the file.**

Using the drop-down list in the Save In box, locate the folder in which you want to save the document. (By default, the My Documents folder is selected.) Double-click the folder's icon to open it.

3. **Name the file.**

In the File Name text box, enter the name you have chosen for your file. You do not need to add the three-character extension; the Office program does that for you.

4. **Save the file, and close the Save As dialog box.**

Click the Save button. Your document is safely stored with the name you entered, in the location you designated. The Save As dialog box closes, returning you to your document.

If you want to save an existing file with a new name, follow the same procedure, deleting the name of the original document in the Save As dialog box and entering a new one. Choose a different location if you want. Your Office program creates a second identical document with the new name and leaves the original document untouched.

Saving a Named File

Once a file has been named, saving changes to it is very simple. Just click the Save button on the Standard toolbar or choose the File menu's Save command. The changed document replaces the old one. Depending upon the speed of your computer, you may see an icon of a computer disk appear briefly in your status bar. With today's faster computers, however, the graphic may appear as a quick blur.

Using AutoRecover

Although it does not take the place of frequent saving, Word and PowerPoint supply a feature called AutoRecover that provides extra insurance against losing data because of a sudden power outage or unexpected computer shut down.

When active, AutoRecover periodically saves a temporary copy of your file. If Word or PowerPoint suddenly close, the data in your file is recovered up to the last AutoRecover save.

Recovering a Document

When the computer is restarted or the application is reopened, AutoRecover automatically lists the files that were running at shut down in the AutoRecover pane to the left of your screen, as shown in Figure 2-10.

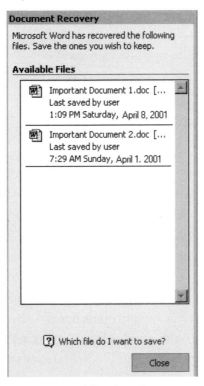

Figure 2-10 The AutoRecover pane.

When the AutoRecover pane appears, recover your file by following these steps:

1. Select a document to recover.

Usually only one document appears in the AutoRecover pane. However, occasionally, you need to choose between several. Each document is listed with its saved name, how it was recovered (saved by author or AutoRecover), and the time of the last saving action. This is usually the same file listed at different save times, as a recent save by author, or as an AutoRecover save. Choosing the most recent file rescues the most of your work. Click the file you want to recover, and the document appears in the document window.

NOTE *If you are unsure which document to select, opening more than one allows you the opportunity to look them over and make comparisons. Click each document in the AutoRecover pane that you want to open. The Office program opens each of them. Access the documents using buttons on the taskbar or the Window menu.*

2. Close the AutoRecover pane.

Click the Close button in the lower right corner of the AutoRecover pane. The pane closes, returning you to your document.

3. Save the document.

It is important to save the recovered document as a named file. Using the Save As dialog box, resave the file with the original document name. If you are asked if you want to replace the original file, select Yes.

Enabling AutoRecover

Word and PowerPoint enable AutoRecover by default. However, if AutoRecover is not running on your computer, you can enable it by following these steps:

1. Open the Save tab of the Options dialog box.

Choose the Tools menu's Options command, and click the Save tab of the Options dialog box. The Save tab reveals the many settings possible in the Office program, as shown in Figure 2-11.

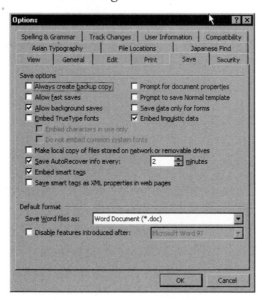

Figure 2-11 The Options dialog box open at the Save tab.

2. **Enable AutoRecover.**

Select the Save AutoRecover Info Every check box. When the box is checked, AutoRecover is enabled. If the box is not checked, AutoRecover is not running.

3. **Close the Options dialog box.**

Click OK to save your changes and close the Options dialog box.

Setting AutoRecover Intervals

Office sets the AutoRecover interval to 10 minutes, by default. If your data is important and difficult to reproduce, set the AutoRecover interval to a shorter time span. Follow these steps:

1. **Open the Save tab of the Options dialog box.**

Choose the Tools menu's Options command, and click the Save tab. The Save tab reveals the many settings possible in the Office program.

2. **Set the AutoRecover interval.**

In the Save AutoRecover Info Every spin box, set the interval for AutoRecover saves. Select the number and type in the interval you want; or use the spin box to determine the number of minutes between AutoRecover saves.

3. **Close the Options dialog box.**

Click OK to save your changes and close the Options dialog box.

NOTE   *AutoRecover is NOT a substitute for regular saving. An AutoRecover save does not save the file to its name and location but merely creates a temporary file that your computer accesses only if your application is suddenly shut down.*

Closing a File

After you finish working with a file, you can close it in either of two ways:

- Choose the File menu's Close command.

- Click the document window's Close button.

NOTE   *If there are two Close buttons in the upper right corner of your program window, the lower one closes the file; the upper one closes the program.*

When all the changes you have made to the file have been saved, the document window showing the file disappears from your screen. However, if there are still changes that need to be saved, a dialog box, as shown in Figure 2-12, appears asking you if you want to save changes. If you click Yes, the Office program saves the document. If you click No, the Office program doesn't save the document, which means you lose any additions or changes.

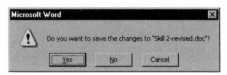

Figure 2-12 The Save Changes dialog box.

Opening an Existing File

After a file has been saved and closed, you can retrieve it using any one of several techniques.

Using the Open Tool or the Open Command

If the application in which a document was created is currently running, it is a simple matter to retrieve the file. Just follow these steps:

1. Open the Open dialog box.

Click the Open button on the Standard toolbar or choose the File menu's Open command. Both techniques display the Open dialog box, as shown in Figure 2-13.

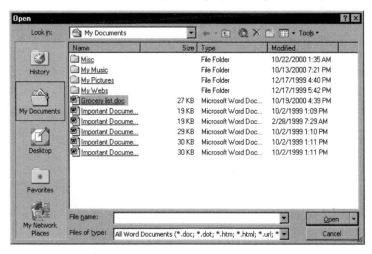

Figure 2-13 The Open dialog box.

2. **Identify the location of the file.**

Using the drop-down list in the Look In box, locate the folder in which you saved the document. (By default, the My Documents folder is selected.) Double-click the folder's icon to open it.

3. **Select the file.**

Click the filename from the open folder.

4. **Open the file, and close the Open dialog box.**

Click the Open button. Your file is safely opened into the program's document window.

Using the Recently Used Files List

If the file you want to retrieve was one of the last four you worked on in that application, an even faster way of retrieving it is to open the File menu and choose the file from the list at the bottom of the menu, as shown in Figure 2-14.

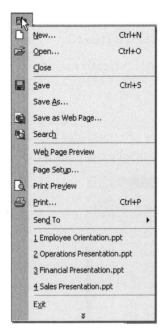

Figure 2-14 The File menu showing the last four files opened.

NOTE   *The Recently Used Files list is also shown on the New pane. To display the New pane, choose the File menu's New command. The pane opens on the right side of your screen.*

Enabling the Recently Used Files List

Office enables the Recently Used Files list by default. However, if there are no recently used files listed at the bottom of the File menu (and you have been working with files), open the Recently Used Files list by following these steps:

1. Open the General tab of the Options dialog box.

Choose the Tools menu's Options command. When the Options dialog box opens, click the General tab, as shown in Figure 2-15.

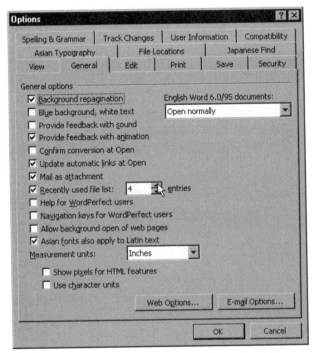

Figure 2-15 The Options dialog box open at the General tab.

2. Enable the Recently Used Files list.

Select the Recently Used Files List check box to enable this feature.

3. Close the Options dialog box.

Click OK to save your changes and close the Options dialog box.

Changing the Number of Files Shown

The number of files shown at the bottom of the File menu is set to four by default. To change that number, follow these steps:

1. Open the General tab of the Options dialog box.

Choose the Tools menu's Options command. When the Options dialog box opens, click the General tab.

2. Set the number of documents.

Use the Recently Used Files List spin box to determine the number of files to be shown on your File menu.

3. Close the Options dialog box.

Click OK to save your changes and close the Options dialog box.

Telling Windows to Open a Document

You don't actually need to start an Office program before opening an existing Office document; if you tell Windows to open a document created by an Office program, it automatically opens the program associated with the document. To do this, you can use the Documents list in the Start menu or use Windows Explorer.

Using the Start Menu

Windows uses the Start menu's Documents list to display recently saved documents. The last 15 documents saved are shown on this list, even if they are not Office files.

If the document you want is on this list, open it by following these steps:

1. Open the Windows Start menu.

Click the Start button on the Windows taskbar. The Start menu is displayed.

2. Open the Documents list.

Click the Documents menu item. A list of 15 recently saved documents appears, as shown in Figure 2-16.

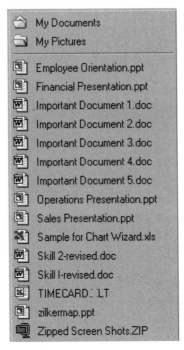

Figure 2-16 The Documents list.

3. Select the file you want to open.

Click the filename. Windows opens the program associated with the file and then opens the document. The Documents list and the Start menu are automatically closed.

Using Windows Explorer

Just as you can open a file from the Documents list, you can also open it from Windows Explorer. To do so, follow these steps:

1. Open Windows Explorer.

Windows Explorer, the file management system within Windows, can be opened in any one of several ways. The most common is to click the Start button, choose Programs, and then choose Windows Explorer. Another way is to right-click the Start button, and choose Explore from the shortcut menu.

TIP   *A lightning-fast keyboard shortcut for opening Windows Explorer works on keyboards that have a Windows key between the Ctrl and Alt keys. Press the Windows key and while holding it down press the E key. Then release both simultaneously. The Windows Explorer window opens immediately.*

2. Display the contents of the folder holding the file.

Use the list in the left pane of the Windows Explorer window to locate the folder where you store the document you want to open. Click the folder icon in the left pane. The folder's contents appear to the right, as shown in Figure 2-17.

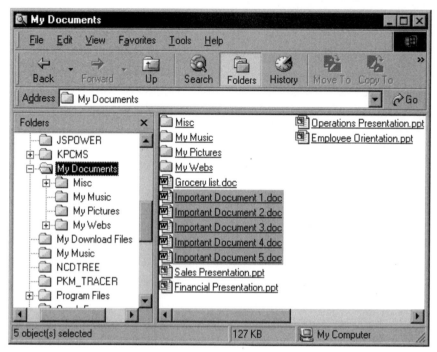

Figure 2-17 The Windows Explorer window.

3. Open the document.

Look for your file in the right pane of the Windows Explorer window. Double-click the document name. Windows opens the application associated with the file and then opens the file itself.

Printing a File

Printing works in essentially the same way in Word, Excel, PowerPoint, and Access. In all these programs, you can use the Print button on the Standard toolbar, which prints one copy of the entire document, or you can choose the File menu's Print command, which opens the Print dialog box, as shown in Figure 2-18, thereby giving you control over how the document prints.

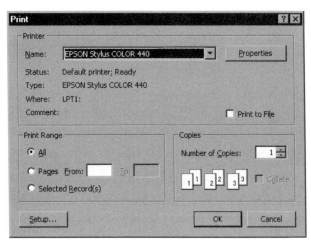

Figure 2-18 The Print dialog box in Access.

NOTE   *To print from any program, you need to first install the printer. Installing merely tells Windows that the printer is connected and established a connection between Windows and the printer. To do this, click the Start button, choose Settings, and then choose Printers. When Windows displays the Printers window, double-click the Add Printer icon. Windows starts the Add A Printer Wizard. Follow its instructions for adding the printer. By the way, if the Printers window already shows the printer you want to use, you don't need to add it.*

Printing in Word, Excel, PowerPoint, and Access

Although similar in all applications, the Print dialog box differs from one to another as it provides print options unique to the individual programs. The following sections are found on the Print dialog box for Word, Excel, PowerPoint, and Access.

Printer Section

The Name text box is the only field in the Printer section that can be changed. The printer initially shown in this box is always the one you have chosen as default; however, you can change to another printer by clicking the drop-down arrow and selecting any printer from those listed. The remainder of the information in the Printer section reflects data on the printer chosen.

Print Range Section

The Print Range section tells the Office program what pages, sheets, slides, or records you want to print. The default Print Range setting is All. All, obviously, prints the entire file.

In Word or PowerPoint, however, you can select to print the one page or slide that is currently active by selecting the Current Page [Slide] check box. In Word, that means that the page that contains the insertion point is the one printed. In PowerPoint, it is the slide that is currently on your screen that is sent to the printer.

Included in the Print Range section is a box that allows you to select specific pages (or slides) for printing. In Excel and Access, you may enter only a single range to send to print; in other words, From: 3 To: 7. However, in Word and PowerPoint, you may indicate individual pages as well as multiple ranges. Indicate ranges with a hyphen between the start and ending pages or slides; for example, *3-7*. Separate individual pages from ranges with a comma but without a space. For example, if you want to print pages one, three through seven, and twelve, you would enter the data like this: *1,3-7,12*, as shown in Figure 2-19. Only those pages (or slides in PowerPoint) print.

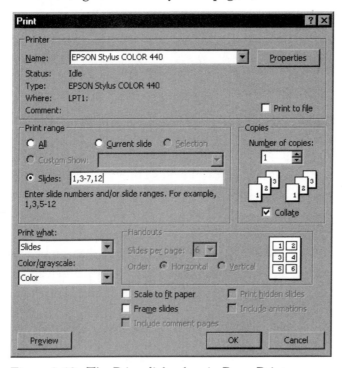

Figure 2-19 The Print dialog box in PowerPoint.

Copies Section

Use the Copies box to specify the number of copies you want. You can type a value in the Copies box. Or, you can use the arrows to spin the numbers up or down to the copy quantity you desire.

The Collate check box allows you to select whether you want multiple copies collated (sorted) as they print or whether you want all copies of each page printed before printing the next page.

Properties Button

Clicking the Properties button in each application's Print dialog box displays another dialog box where you can set your printer's parameters for that specific print job. Settings such as quality of print, type of paper, and color settings are unique to the printer you have installed and differs from one printer to another, as shown in Figure 2-20. Check your printer documentation for more information.

Figure 2-20 The Properties dialog box for an Epson printer.

Printing in Outlook

Printing in Outlook works differently from printing in other Office programs because the different Outlook items (e-mail messages, calendar appointments, notes, and tasks) supply different information.

As in printing with other Office programs, however, you can print the open or selected Outlook item by clicking the Print toolbar button. For example, if you are working within the Inbox, perhaps reviewing your e-mail messages, clicking Print prints the open or selected e-mail message.

If you want more control over how some item is printed, choose the File menu's Print command. Then when Outlook displays the Print dialog box, use its buttons and boxes to describe how Outlook should print the item, as shown in Figure 2-21. The paragraphs that follow briefly discuss what printing options you have available for Outlook items.

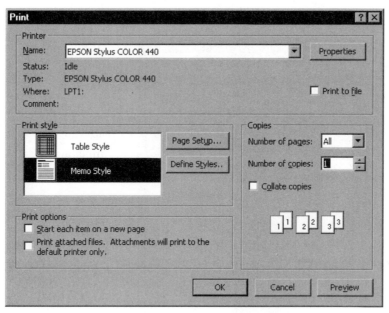

Figure 2-21 The Print dialog box for Inbox.

Printer Section

The Printer section of Outlook's Print dialog box works like the Printer section in other Office program Print dialog boxes. Your default printer is shown in the Name box. To change to another printer, select its name from the drop-down list.

Print Style Section

The Print Style section presents you with one or more styles with which you can print your data. For example, in Calendar, if you select the Weekly Style, the appointments in your calendar print out in a one-page-per-week style; if you select Daily Style, you get a one-page-per-day layout.

Also within the Print Style section are buttons for Page Setup and Define Styles. Page Setup allows you to change margins or configure the data to predetermined paper sizes. For example, you could format Calendar to print on paper specifically designed for your organizer.

The Define Styles button allows you to tweak the Print Styles to your preference.

Copies Section

Use the Number Of Pages drop-down list to select whether you want to print all pages (select All) or whether you want to print odd or even pages (select Odd or Even). If you want to print a document double-sided but do not have a printer that will automatically do so, you can print the odd pages and then turn them over and insert them back into your printer so that the even pages print on the back. Run a test with sample pages to see whether you need to rearrange the first set for correct printing.

Also, in the Copies section, you choose the number of copies you want to print. Click the Number Of Copies spin box to select the existing number and then enter a new number; or, you can use the arrows to spin the numbers up or down to the quantity you desire.

The Collate check box allows you to select whether you want multiple copies collated (sorted) as they are printed or whether you want all copies of each page to be printed before printing the next page.

Print Options Section for Inbox and Notes

The two check boxes in the Print Options section allow you to select print preferences. Start Each Item On A New Page, obviously, causes each note or e-mail message to print on its own page or pages. Print Attached Files prints any files that have been attached to e-mail.

Print Range Section for Contacts, Tasks, and Calendar Functions

In the Contacts and Tasks dialog boxes, the Print Range section consists of two option buttons, as shown in Figure 2-22. As you would expect, All Items prints every Contact or Task entry in your list, while Only Selected Items prints only those items you have selected prior to opening the Print dialog box.

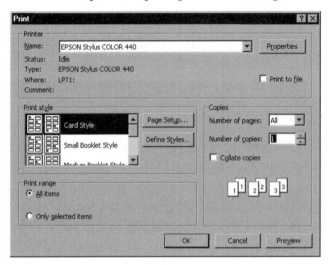

Figure 2-22 The Print dialog box for Contacts.

In the Calendar function, the Print Range section allows you to choose two dates to indicate which Calendar pages you want to print, as shown in Figure 2-23.

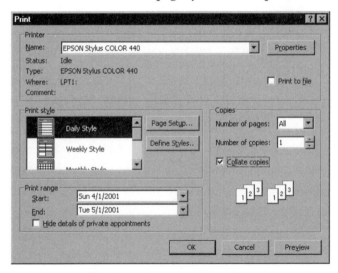

Figure 2-23 The Print dialog box for Calendar.

Skill 3

USE OUTLOOK FOR EASY ORGANIZATION

Featuring:

- The Outlook Shortcuts Bar
- Using E-Mail
- Using Calendar
- Using Contacts
- Using Tasks

Microsoft Outlook is the perfect tool for keeping track of appointments, contacts, and the things you've got to do as well as sending, receiving, and managing e-mail. And, when Outlook is used in conjunction with others on your network, it develops additional depth. In this skill, we discuss the Outlook Shortcuts bar and the four primary functions in Outlook.

TIP   *It is a good idea to keep Outlook open and minimized throughout your computer session. With Outlook open, you can receive immediate notification of the arrival of e-mail messages and have instantaneous access to your Calendar and Contacts list.*

The Outlook Shortcuts Bar

Predominant on the Outlook screen is the toolbar that runs vertically on the left side of the document area. This bar contains shortcut buttons divided into groups for convenience. The Outlook Shortcuts bar contains buttons for Inbox, Contacts, Calendar, and Tasks, as shown in Figure 3-1. Clicking any one of these buttons immediately takes you to the screen for that function.

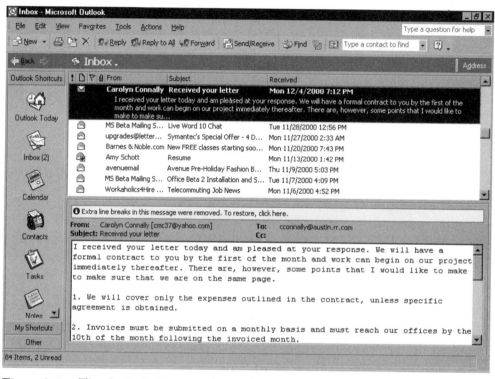

Figure 3-1   The Outlook Shortcuts bar and the Inbox screen.

At the bottom of the bar, by default, are two other groups, which open when the group button is clicked: My Shortcuts and Other. The My Shortcuts bar contains buttons for Drafts, Inbox, Sent Items, Outbox, and Deleted Items. Additional buttons may be added to this bar, as you want. The Other bar provides convenient access to My Computer, My Documents, and Favorites. Just like the My Shortcuts bar, additional buttons can be added to conveniently connect you to locations on your computer system or on the Web.

Customizing the Outlook Shortcuts Bar

To customize the Outlook Shortcuts bar to your personal preferences, you can add or remove any buttons as well as add or remove any shortcut bars.

Adding New Shortcut Buttons

To add shortcut buttons to any of the shortcut groups, follow these steps:

1. **Select the group to which you want to add a shortcut button.**

   The various shortcut groups are shown by rectangular buttons within the Outlook bar area. Click the group of your choice to make it active.

2. **Select Outlook Bar Shortcut.**

   Right-click the Outlook Shortcuts bar and choose Outlook Bar Shortcut from the shortcut menu.

3. **Designate the shortcut item.**

   Using the list in the Add To Outlook Bar dialog box, locate and select the folder or file for which you want to create a shortcut.

4. **Click OK.**

   A button representing your selection appears on the bar.

Removing Shortcut Buttons

Shortcut buttons are just as easily removed from the Outlook Shortcut bar. Just follow these steps:

1. **Right-click the shortcut button you want to remove.**

   Right-clicking the shortcut button opens a shortcut menu.

2. **Select the Remove From Shortcut Bar command.**

   From the shortcut menu, locate and click the Remove From Shortcut Bar command to select it.

3. **Acknowledge removal of the button.**

   When the Outlook dialog box appears asking if you are sure you want to remove the shortcut, click OK.

Adding New Outlook Shortcut Bar Groups

You can easily add as many groups as you want. Follow these steps:

1. **Right-click any shortcut group button.**

   Right-clicking any rectangular group button on the Outlook Shortcuts bar opens a shortcut menu.

2. **Select the Add New Group command.**

   From the shortcut menu, select the Add New Group command. A new group button appears at the bottom of the Outlook Shortcuts bar.

3. **Rename the new group button.**

   When the new group button appears, it is named New Group and is highlighted for renaming. All you have to do is to begin typing the name of your new group and press the Enter key.

Once you have created a new group, you can add any shortcut buttons you want, as described above.

Using E-Mail

Of all of Outlook's functions, the most used is the sending and receiving of e-mail. The Inbox is where incoming e-mail is displayed as well as being the starting point for outgoing e-mail and e-mail file management. Outlook's Inbox works very similarly to most e-mail systems but has the advantage of convenient interaction with the rest of Office's programs.

In this section, we discuss sending and receiving e-mail messages as well as how to manage your e-mail files.

Creating a New E-Mail Message

E-mail is such a convenient way to communicate. It is certainly faster than U.S. Postal Service mail and is a lot cheaper. If you are a new e-mail user, you can be assured that once you are familiar with using e-mail you will never want to go back to the other communication media.

To send an e-mail message, follow these steps:

1. **Open a new message form.**

   Click the first button on the Standard toolbar of the Outlook Inbox screen. An Untitled – Message form appears, as shown in Figure 3-2.

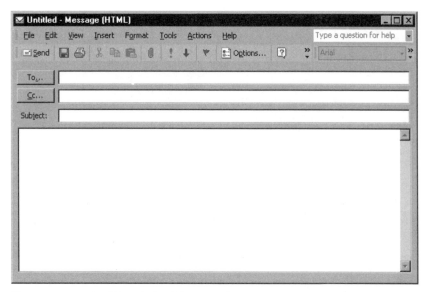

Figure 3-2   An Untitled – Message form.

2. Enter the e-mail address of the person or persons to whom you want to send a message.

There are several ways to enter the e-mail address of your message's recipient:

- Type it in—This is a very simple way to enter the e-mail address. Of course you have to know it, correctly and in full. For some e-mail addresses that is not a problem. For others, with more complicated addresses, it may be a challenge. If you want to send your message to more than one person, place a comma between each address leaving no blank spaces.

- Pull it from your Contacts list—If your recipient's e-mail address is listed in your Contacts list, simply click the To button. The Select Names box, as shown in Figure 3-3, appears, and you can select the recipient from the Name list box, and then click the To button. The recipient's name appears in the Message Recipients box on the right side of the window. Repeat for additional recipients, and then click OK. Outlook places the name or names in the To box for you.

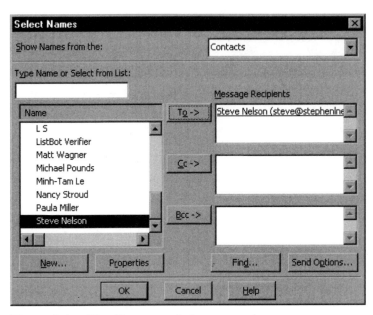

Figure 3-3 The Contacts window.

- Copy and paste—If you have access to the recipient's address from a document, a Web site, or another e-mail—any place you can highlight and copy it—then you can use the copy-and-paste technique, which eliminates potential mistakes. Just go to the document containing the e-mail address, highlight it, and click the Copy button on the toolbar, if available. Then move back to the Untitled – Message form and click in the To box. Click the Paste button on the Standard toolbar. The address appears in the text box. If you locate the address in a document or program that does not make the Copy button available to you, use the Ctrl+C keystroke combination to copy the item. If you want to add multiple addresses, place a comma between each address.

3. Enter carbon copy addresses.

Enter carbon copy (Cc) addresses using any of the same techniques described above.

NOTE *The terminology* carbon copy *comes from the days when carbon paper was used to make a copy of a memo or letter to send to someone other than the direct recipient as a way of including them in the information loop. Here, it also means that a copy is being sent to an individual other than the direct recipient. Placing the address in the Cc box indicates that the message is just for their information.*

4. Enter a subject.

Entering a subject is not an absolute necessity. However, it is considered the polite thing to do. If your recipient is a busy person (and who isn't?), they may need information on what the message is about in order to prioritize their time.

5. Write your message.

The message text box provides you space to write a message of even great length to your addressee.

6. Send your message.

If your message is complete, click the Send button in the upper left of the message window to send it to the addressee.

NOTE *For an e-mail message to be sent, there must first be an Internet connection. If you have a dial-up Internet connection, you must establish the connection before the message is sent. If you have a dial-up Internet connection, clicking the Send button puts the message into the Outbox where it stays until the connection is established.*

TIP *By default, the message is typically sent across the Internet immediately. However, if you see messages in your Outbox (found in the My Shortcuts group), a setting may have been changed causing Outlook to hold the messages before sending. You can send any held messages by clicking the Send And Receive button on the Inbox Standard toolbar. Then change the setting by choosing the Tools menu's Option command and clicking the Mail Setup tab. Select the Send Immediately When Connected check box.*

Attaching a File

E-mail is frequently used today to send files across the Internet. Obviously, this method is faster than mail and cleaner than fax. If you want to attach a file to your e-mail message, just follow these steps:

1. Open the Insert File dialog box.

When you have completed your e-mail message and before you click the Send button, click the Insert File button on the Standard toolbar (it has a picture of a paper clip). The Insert File dialog box appears, as shown in Figure 3-4.

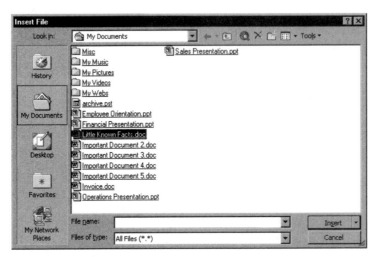

Figure 3-4   The Insert File dialog box.

2. Select the file you want to attach.

Using the list in the Insert File dialog box, locate the file you want to attach and click to select it.

3. Attach the file.

Click the Insert button in the lower right corner of the Insert File dialog box. The file is now attached to your message.

Receiving Messages

When you start Outlook, the function that opens first is usually Outlook's Inbox, as shown in Figure 3-5. The most commonly used function, Inbox provides a split window so that you can see the list of e-mails you have received in the top half, or Mailbox screen, and the selected message in the lower portion, the Message screen. Additionally, by default, a preview of the message—the first three lines—is also shown in the mailbox on unread items. If you double-click a message in the mailbox, it opens into a standalone window for easier viewing. Messages that have not been opened appear in the top half in bold type. Once you have opened a message and kept it open for a few seconds, it is considered read and is listed without the bold type effect.

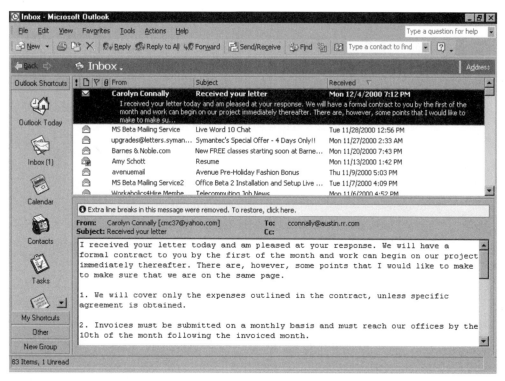

Figure 3-5   Outlook's Inbox.

Responding to Messages

When you receive a message, you may want to respond, just as you would with mail received through the U.S. Postal Service. In Outlook, it is easy to reply to the sender of the message, reply so that all individuals to whom the message was sent receive your response, or forward the message to someone else. The Reply, Reply To All and Forward buttons are found on the toolbar of the Inbox and the standalone message screen, as shown in Figure 3-6.

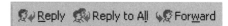

Figure 3-6   The Reply, Reply To All, and Forward buttons.

Reply

When you click the Reply button, a message form appears with the subject of the original message referenced in the title bar. Outlook automatically places the e-mail address of the original sender, now your recipient, in the To box, and the sender's original text appears, for reference, in the message area. All you need to do is type your response (above the referenced text) and click the Send button.

Reply To All

Clicking this button produces the exact same result as the Reply button except that your response is sent, not to just the sender, but to any other individuals to whom the original message was also addressed. Make very certain that you want all of the recipients of the original message to see your reply before you use this option.

Forward

When you want to send the original message on to someone else, perhaps with a note from yourself, click the Forward button. Once the message form appears on your screen, enter the e-mail address of the person or persons to whom you want to forward the e-mail, using the techniques identified in the "Creating a New E-Mail Message" section. Keep in mind that whenever a message is forwarded, all of the address information from the original message is included with it. And after several forwards, the message becomes unwieldy with data that is no longer important. You can select all of the unimportant data in the message area of the form and delete it; thus, making the message far simpler and easier to read.

Maintaining E-Mail Files

E-mail maintenance is just like any other file maintenance. You carefully file away those that you feel should be kept for a while and get rid of any messages that you do not want to keep. The following sections tell you how to do just that, and more.

Delete

For even a casual e-mail user, messages can mount up very quickly. If you don't make a habit of deleting them regularly, you will soon have a very full Inbox. Once you have read an e-mail message (or have viewed the preview) and determined that you want to get rid of it, follow these steps:

1. **Select the message.**

   You can select the message by clicking it in the mailbox or double-clicking it to open it.

2. Click the Delete button.

A Delete button appears in the Standard toolbar of the Inbox as well as of the Message window. The icon on it looks like a large, freeform X. All you have to do is click the Delete button and the message is removed from your Inbox.

NOTE   *Do not confuse the Delete button on the toolbar with the Close button in the upper right corner of the Outlook window. The latter closes down Outlook entirely.*

Moving a File to a Folder

If you want to store the e-mail permanently, follow these steps:

1. Select the message.

Select the message by clicking it in the Inbox's mailbox pane.

2. Choose the File menu's Save As command.

Click the File menu, and select Save As.

3. Locate the folder, and save the file.

Using the list in the Save As dialog box, as shown in Figure 3-7, locate the folder in which you want to store the message. Click the Save button.

Figure 3-7   The Save As dialog box.

4. Delete the file from the Inbox.

Even though you have saved the file to the folder where you want to store it, the file still appears in your Inbox until you delete it. Select the message, if necessary, and click the Delete toolbar button.

Sorting Inbox Messages

Sometimes you may want to keep your e-mail in the Inbox, at least for a while. If a large number accumulate, however, finding the one message you want to refer to may be confusing. Outlook makes it easy to sort your messages so that you can easily find the one you want.

Each of the headings in the Inbox is also a sorting key. When you click a heading button, Outlook sorts the messages by that key. For example, if you want to find a message from a particular sender, click the From heading, as shown in Figure 3-8. Outlook sorts all your messages alphabetically by sender. Then scroll through the messages from the specific sender to find the one you want.

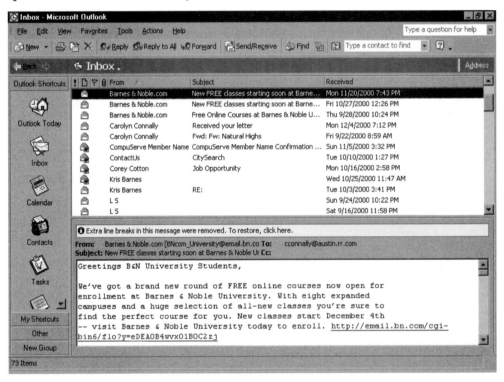

Figure 3-8   The Inbox with e-mail messages sorted by sender.

NOTE   *By default, your messages are sorted by date of receipt. This is a good way to keep your messages because that puts the newest ones on top, right where you can find them.*

Searching for a Message

Another way of locating a particular message is to use the Find feature of Outlook. To do this, follow these steps:

1. Open the Search field.

Clicking the Find button, located on the Standard toolbar, displays Search fields at the top of the mailbox screen, as shown in Figure 3-9.

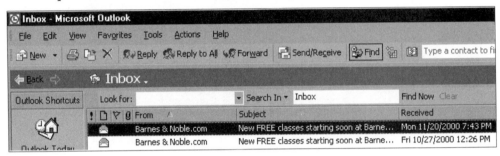

Figure 3-9   The Inbox with the Search fields displayed.

2. Enter text.

In the Look For box, type a word or phrase that is in the message you are looking for.

3. Start the search.

Click the Find Now button. Outlook scans every one of your e-mail messages and returns those that contain that word or phrase.

4. Open the message.

Open a message from the search results by double-clicking it.

Using Calendar

The Outlook Calendar is a highly flexible tool that can take the place of your pocket planner or work in conjunction with it.

Setting Calendar Configuration

Your Outlook Calendar can be set to display a daily, weekly, or full-month configuration. Keep the setting at the view most convenient for you, and change it as needed.

Daily View

To display the Daily view, click the Day button on the Calendar Standard toolbar. The Daily view shows all hours of the day in 30-minute increments, as shown in Figure 3-10. Typical business hours are shown more brightly than the other hours to help prevent you from scheduling an appointment for 3:30 in the morning by mistake. This is a good view for keeping track of your schedule. There is space to easily read the notation.

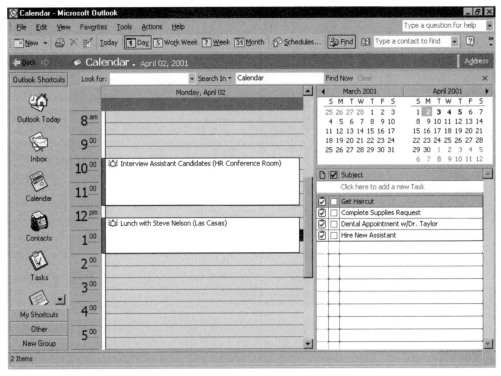

Figure 3-10 The Outlook Calendar in Daily view.

Also included in the Daily view are small full-month calendars for the current and upcoming months. A list of your tasks is shown as well (see the section "Using Tasks," later in this skill).

Work Week View

To display the Work Week view, click the Work Week button on the Standard toolbar. This view shows all hours for a typical work week of five days. The small full-month calendars and the Tasks list are in this view, as well, leaving very little room for appointment notations, as shown in Figure 3-11. The Work Week view is probably best used as a broad reference of your weekly schedule.

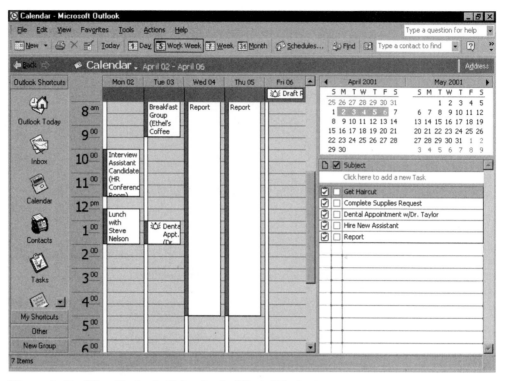

Figure 3-11 The Outlook Calendar in Work Week view.

NOTE *If your work week is not typical, the days displayed in the Work Week view can be changed by selecting the Tools menu's Options command and then clicking the Calendar Options button in the Options dialog box.*

Week View

The Week view displays all seven weekdays in a block format that does not show hours, the small full-month calendars, and the Tasks list, as shown in Figure 3-12. Again, this is a good summary view for a really busy person or as the primary view for the individual who does not make extensive appointment notations. To display the Week view, click the Week button on the Standard toolbar.

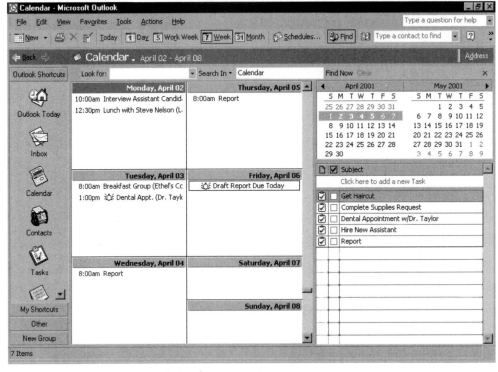

Figure 3-12 The Outlook Calendar in Week view.

Month View

In this view, Outlook fills the display space with a full calendar month, as shown in Figure 3-13. Appointments and notations are shown in abbreviated form. Previous and upcoming months may be viewed by scrolling the screen up or down as needed.

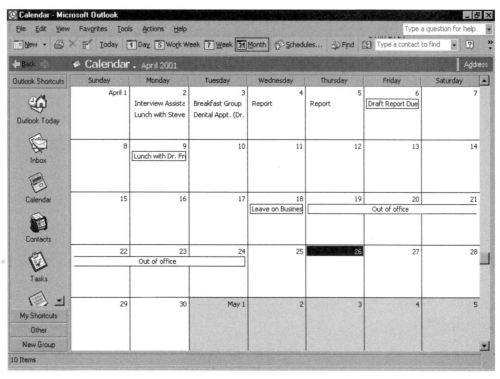

Figure 3-13 The Outlook Calendar in Month view.

Setting Appointments

Keeping track of the things you have to do is what Calendar is all about. For our purposes, we consider an appointment any notation that you need to make to remind you to do something, go somewhere, see someone, or to be aware of something. In other words, you can use an appointment to remind you of your spouse's birthday, or remind you of that big important meeting with a client, or indicate that it is payday. However you use the Appointment function, you will find it convenient and easy.

NOTE   *The accuracy of your Calendar greatly depends upon the accuracy of your system's clock. If your system clock is not correct, open the Date/Time dialog box by double-clicking on the time on your taskbar. Then set the correct date and time, and click OK.*

Creating an Appointment

To create an appointment, follow these steps:

1. **Open a new appointment form.**

   From the Calendar screen in Outlook, click the New button on the Standard toolbar. An Untitled – Appointment form appears, as shown in Figure 3-14.

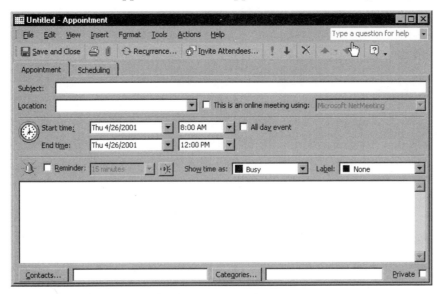

Figure 3-14 The Untitled – Appointment form.

2. **Enter the appointment subject and location.**

   In the text boxes provided, enter a subject and a location for your appointment. Keep in mind that, depending upon which Calendar view you use, only the first words (or even the first few letters) of your appointment subject are shown. So you want to keep the subject and location entries very brief and to the point. Rather than enter directions to a location in the Location box, use the text box at the bottom of the screen for directions and merely enter *There* or *Her Office* in the Location box.

3. **Enter start and end times.**

   Both the Start Time and the End Time boxes have drop-down lists for the date and for the time. When you click the Date drop-down arrow, a small calendar appears. Click the date on the calendar or use the arrows in the upper corners of the calendar to scroll to another month, and then select the date. Clicking the drop-down arrow of the Time box provides you with AM and PM times in 30-minute increments. Just click the appropriate time.

If the appointment you want to set is a day-long event, your mother's birthday for example, select the All Day Event check box. The Start Time and End Time boxes disappear, leaving only the date. The All Day Event selection provides a calendar notation for the entire day but does not prevent other appointments from being made.

4. **Enter reminder criteria.**

You can ask Outlook Calendar to remind you of an appointment by selecting the Reminder check box. Then use the drop-down list box to specify when you want to be reminded. You may choose to be reminded anywhere from two weeks before the appointment to the appointment time itself.

5. **Enter the Show Time As information.**

If you are working on a local network configured so that individual calendars are interactive, indicate whether the time you are setting aside for this appointment is Free, Tentative, Busy, or Out-Of-The-Office. Therefore, if others are trying to schedule a meeting, interacting with your Calendar tells them whether you are available to them during that time or not.

6. **Optionally, enter a label.**

The Label box allows you an immediate indication of the importance of the event. Click the drop-down arrow, and choose from the selections provided.

7. **Enter any other pertinent information.**

Use the text box at the bottom of the window to enter any explanation or descriptive information you may need for the appointment.

8. **Save and close.**

Click the Save And Close button on the Standard toolbar. The Appointment dialog box closes and returns you to the Calendar screen.

Setting a Recurring Appointment

Whether it is the weekly staff meeting or your twice-weekly massage, Outlook makes it easy for you to set up recurring appointments. You just set it once, put in the parameters, and wait for the reminders. Follow these steps:

1. **Open a new appointment form.**

From the Calendar screen in Outlook, click the New button on the Standard toolbar. An Untitled – Appointment form appears, as shown in Figure 3-14.

2. Enter the appointment subject and location.

In the text boxes provided, enter a subject and a location for your appointment. Keep in mind that, depending upon which Calendar view you use, only the first words (or even the first few letters) of your appointment subject are shown. So you want to keep the subject and location entries very brief and to the point. Rather than enter directions to a location in the Location box, use the text box at the bottom of the screen for directions and merely enter *There* or *Her Office* in the Location box.

3. Enter recurrence parameters.

Click the Recurrence button on the Standard toolbar. The Appointment Recurrence dialog box opens, as shown in Figure 3-15.

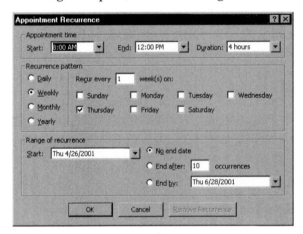

Figure 3-15 The Appointment Recurrence dialog box.

Enter the appointment parameters as follows:

- Appointment Time—Enter the start time and end time of the appointment. The duration automatically configures.

- Recurrence Pattern—First indicate whether the appointment recurs Daily, Weekly, Monthly, or Yearly; the appropriate choices are then shown to the right. Choose the settings that appropriately configure your appointment.

- Range Of Recurrence—Enter the start date by clicking the Start drop-down arrow. Locate the appropriate calendar by using the Forward and Back buttons to the left and right of the calendar. Then click the appropriate start date. Choose the appropriate end format, and enter the information required.

4. **Click OK.**

Click OK to return to the Appointment dialog box.

5. **Enter reminder criteria.**

You can ask Outlook Calendar to remind you of each occurrence of the appointment by selecting the Reminder check box. Then use the drop-down list box to specify when you want to be reminded. You may choose to be reminded anywhere from two weeks before the appointment to the appointment time itself.

6. **Enter the Show Time As information.**

If you are working on a local network configured so that individual calendars are interactive, indicate whether the time you are setting aside for this appointment is Free, Tentative, Busy or Out-Of-The-Office. Therefore, if others are trying to sched-ule a meeting, interacting with your Calendar tells them whether you are available to them during that time or not.

7. **Optionally, enter a label.**

The Label box allows you an immediate indication of the nature of the event. Click the drop-down arrow, and choose from the selections provided.

8. **Enter any other pertinent information.**

Use the text box at the bottom of the window to enter any explanation or descrip-tive information you may need for the appointment.

9. **Save and close.**

Click the Save And Close button on the Standard toolbar. The Appointment dia-log box closes and returns you to the Calendar screen.

Using the Reminder

If you have indicated that you want to be reminded of an appointment, a reminder appears on your screen at the time you indicated, as shown in Figure 3-16.

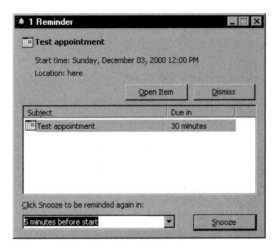

Figure 3-16 The Reminder box.

You can respond to the message box in any one of three ways:

- Open Item—Clicking the Open Item button opens the appointment's dialog box so that you can retrieve any information in the text box or refresh your memory on the appointment.

- Dismiss—Acknowledge the appointment by clicking the Dismiss button, in which case, the message box closes.

- Snooze—If you want to be reminded again of the appointment, set the interval at which you want the reminder to reappear and click the Snooze button.

Using Contacts

Outlook provides you with an Address Book, which is as accessible as your computer and is easily modified to reflect changes in a contact's information, as shown in Figure 3-17.

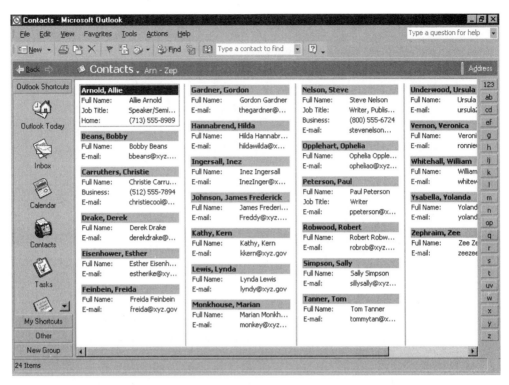

Figure 3-17 The Contacts window.

The Contacts list saves you from having to type in addresses when you want to send e-mails to those on your list (see "Creating a New E-Mail Message" earlier in this skill). It can be printed in any of several useful formats, and it can be used as the source data for mail-merge functions in Word.

Entering a New Contact

There are two ways to enter a new contact in your list: automatically from an e-mail or by manually entering the contact information.

Automatically from an E-Mail

When you receive an e-mail from someone whom you would like to add to your Contacts list, right-click their name in the Message box and choose Add To Contacts from the shortcut menu. In the Contact dialog box, enter additional information on the contact if you want. Then click Save And Close. The individual is added to your Contacts list.

Manually Enter the Information

To enter contact information manually, follow these steps:

1. **Open a new contact form.**

   From the Contacts screen in Outlook, click the New button on the Standard toolbar. An Untitled – Contact form appears, as shown in Figure 3-18.

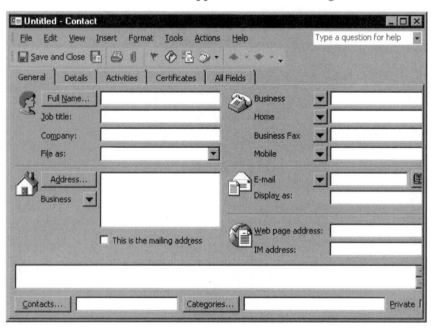

Figure 3-18 An Untitled – Contact form.

2. **Enter the contact information.**

There is a field in the Untitled – Contact form to enter just about any information you may want to keep on an individual or organization. The General tab asks for the most commonly used information while the Details tab asks for more specific data. Enter the information you want to store.

3. **Save and close.**

Clicking the Save And Close button on the Standard toolbar saves the information to your Contacts file and returns you to the Contacts screen.

Locating a Contact

On the right side of the Contacts window are alphabetical links to the Contacts list (see Figure 3-17). Clicking the appropriate letter brings names beginning with that letter into view. Open the contact by double-clicking the highlighted name.

Generating an E-Mail Message from Contacts

To generate an e-mail message from a Contact window, follow these steps:

1. **Open the Contact window.**

From the Contacts screen, locate the listing for the contact to whom you want to send an e-mail message and double-click to open the Contact window.

2. **Click the New Message To Contact button.**

Clicking the New Message To Contact button on the Standard toolbar, as shown in Figure 3-19, opens an Untitled – Message form with your contact's e-mail address already entered.

Figure 3-19   The New Message To Contact button on the Standard toolbar.

If you want to add more addresses to this message, click the To button and add new addresses as mentioned in "Creating a New E-Mail Message" earlier in this skill.

3. **Complete the message.**

Enter in the subject and the message content.

4. Send the message.

Clicking the Send button on the Standard toolbar sends your message to your recipients.

Using Tasks

The Tasks function of Outlook is a handy place to keep your to-do list. Just add tasks to your list as they occur and the Tasks list keeps track of them until you mark them as completed. Using the Tasks list, as shown in Figure 3-20, keeps all the things you have to do in front of you so that something doesn't slip through the cracks.

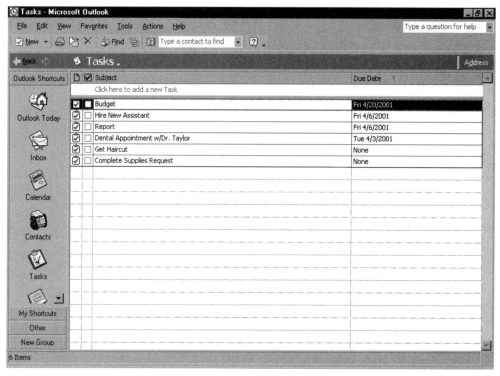

Figure 3-20 The Tasks window.

What's more, Outlook's Tasks function helps you stay on track. Your list is displayed on the Tasks screen and on most of the Calendar views as well. You can also add reminders to your tasks to help keep you on schedule.

Entering a New Task

For the most effective use of this function, add tasks to your list as soon as the need develops. To do this, follow these steps:

1. Open an Untitled – Task form.

From the Tasks screen, click the New Task button on the Standard toolbar. The Untitled – Task form appears, as shown in Figure 3-21.

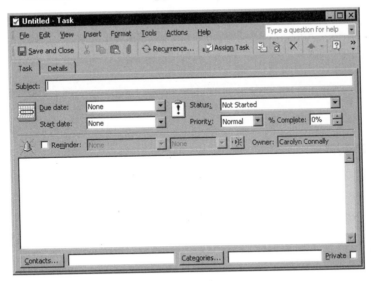

Figure 3-21 The Untitled – Task form.

2. Enter the task information.

Complete the following fields to establish the project parameters:

- Subject—Enter a simple name to identify the project to you. Save lengthy descriptions for the text box at the bottom of the form.

- Due Date—Click the drop-down arrow to display a calendar. Click the appropriate due date or use the arrows in the upper right and upper left to scroll to another month and select the date.

- Start Date—Enter the first day you intend to work on this task.

- Status—Indicate the condition of the task by choosing from the selections in the drop-down list box.

- Priority—Plan your time by indicating whether the task is of Low, Normal, or High priority. Select one of the categories from the drop-down list box.

- % Complete—Track your progress by indicating the percentage of the project that has been completed. Type in a number, or use the spin buttons.

- Reminder—Set an alarm clock to remind you when time is growing short. Click in the selection box and then set the day and time.

- Owner—Enter the name of the person with the ultimate responsibility to see that the task is completed. You may want to leave your name in place, or list the individual who assigned the task to you.

3. Save and close.

Click the Save And Close button on the Standard toolbar to add the task to your list.

Maintaining Tasks

The information you enter in the Task form can be adjusted at any time. Certainly as a large task proceeds, you will want to update the percentage completed. To reopen the Task dialog box, double-click the task in the Tasks list or in Calendar and the form is displayed for you to edit.

Deleting a Completed Task

Tasks that have been completed may be listed as such by opening the Task dialog box and clicking the Mark As Complete button on the Standard toolbar. The task is then shown as complete by a check mark in the selection box next to the task, as shown in Figure 3-22. In the Tasks list, there will also be a line drawn through the completed task.

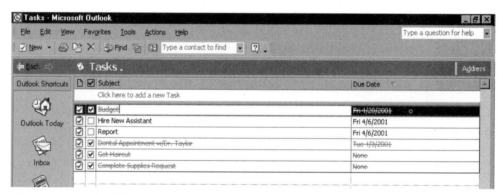

Figure 3-22 The Tasks list in the Daily Calendar view with completed tasks shown checked off.

To delete a completed task, open the Task dialog box by double-clicking it and then click the Delete button on the Standard toolbar.

Skill 4

USE WORD FOR DOCUMENT GENERATION

Featuring:

- Entering and Editing Text
- Automatic Editing with AutoCorrect and AutoText
- Formatting Your Word Document
- Spelling and Grammar Checking
- Using the Thesaurus

Microsoft Word is a powerful tool for many everyday business activities. However, it is Word's primary usage—the generation, editing, and formatting of text documents—that we are discussing in this skill.

Entering and Editing Text

Entering and editing text is what Word is all about. The ease with which this can be done makes Word an essential business tool. We are discussing entering and editing text as separate sections here but in Word they form an almost seamless process.

Just Type to Enter Text

Simply put, to enter text, just type. Whatever you type is entered in your Word document. The newly typed text appears in your document at the position of the insertion point, a small, pulsating, vertical bar, as shown in Figure 4-1. You can move the insertion point to a new position within existing text, merely by clicking your mouse where you want it located.

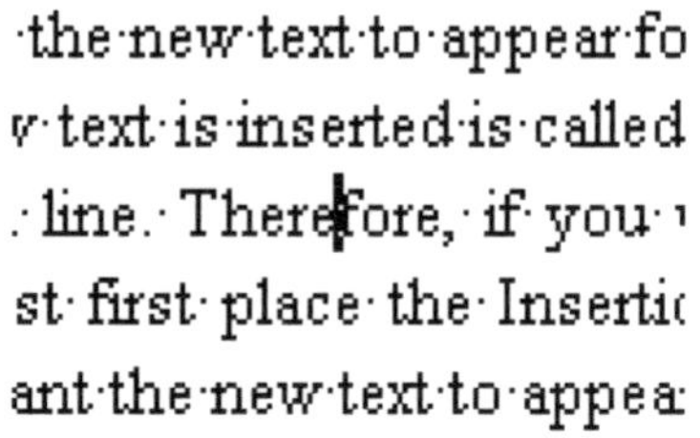

```
·the·new·text·to·appear·fo
v·text·is·inserted·is·called
·line.·Therefore,·if·you·1
st·first·place·the·Insertic
ant·the·new·text·to·appea:
```

Figure 4-1   The insertion point.

Entering text in the midst of existing text causes the program to automatically adjust the lines of type to allow for the new data.

NOTE   *If the text overtypes the existing text instead of moving it ahead, Word's overtype feature is turned on. To turn it off, double-click the OVR abbreviation in the status bar of your Word screen or press the Insert key.*

When text reaches the end of a line, it automatically wraps to the next line. Pressing the Enter key causes the insertion point to return to the left margin, creating a new paragraph.

Entering Text Using Speech Recognition

We heard that it was coming and now it's here! Speech Recognition is a part of Office! Speech Recognition means that you can speak into a computer microphone and Word will translate your spoken word into the written word.

Up until now, Speech Recognition software was something that you bought separately from any one of several software developers and added to your system. It has primarily been used by those for whom typing on a keyboard and clicking a mouse is a physical challenge, or by physicians, pathologists, researchers, and others who need to keep hands free while entering data. Now, however, it is available to all users of Word.

You will need speakers and a microphone. Headset microphones provide the best results. You can find relatively inexpensive headset microphones at your local electronics or office supply store.

Depending upon the choices you made when installing Office, you may need to install the Speech Recognition engine. Also, you will need to train the Speech Recognition software to recognize your voice.

Installing Speech Recognition

Choose the Tools menu's Speech command. The Speech Recognition installation verification box appears asking whether you want to install Speech Recognition, as shown in Figure 4-2. When asked to do so, insert your Office CD into the CD-ROM drive. A progress meter shows the progress of the installation. You will need to restart your computer before the new software can take effect.

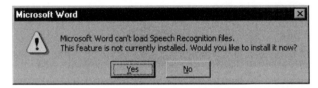

Figure 4-2   The Speech Recognition installation verification box.

Establishing Microphone Settings

Before you train the software to recognize your voice, you must adjust the microphone. Office provides a wizard to help you with that. In Control Panel, click the Speech icon to open the Speech Properties dialog box, as shown in Figure 4-3.

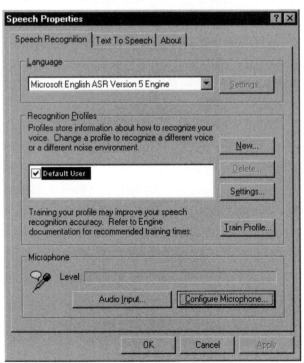

Figure 4-3   The Speech Properties dialog box.

Click the Configure Microphone button to start the Microphone Wizard, as shown in Figure 4-4. Follow the wizard's instructions to establish the correct microphone settings.

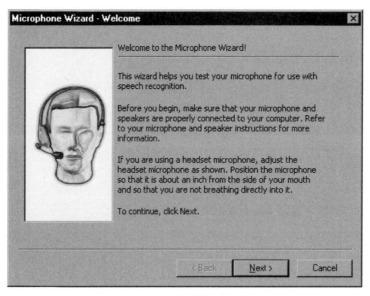

Figure 4-4 The first screen of the Microphone Wizard.

Training the Speech Engine

Now the Speech Recognition software must record your voice reading several phrases so that it can recognize your speaking style and pronunciation. In the Speech Properties dialog box, click the Train Profile button. The Training Wizard leads you through the process, just follow the onscreen instructions. Be sure to allow enough time to complete this process.

Once you have trained the Speech engine, you can open the Speech Recognition feature by choosing the Tools menu's Speech command.

Editing Text

After entering text, you may find that you want to change what you have typed. Maybe you need to correct a misspelled word or rewrite a sentence. You may want to add more text or remove some. Each of these editing techniques is easy to accomplish.

Replacing Text

In order to replace text, first select the text that you want to change (see the sidebar "Selecting Text"). Once text is highlighted, just begin typing the replacement text. With your first keystroke, the highlighted text is replaced with the new.

Removing Text

When you enter text that you do not want to keep, you can easily remove it. Several techniques can be used, depending upon the circumstances. If, as you type, you enter a character in error, or just change your mind, pressing the Backspace key deletes the character to the *left* of your insertion point. This is fast and effective for small deletions.

The Delete key works very much like the Backspace key; however, it removes text to the *right* of the insertion point. Therefore, to use this technique, you need to position the insertion point to the left of the text you want to delete.

If the correction you want to make is more than a few characters, you may want to select the text, as shown in Figure 4-5, and then use either the Backspace key or Delete key to remove all the selected text. When text is selected, both of these keys perform the same action.

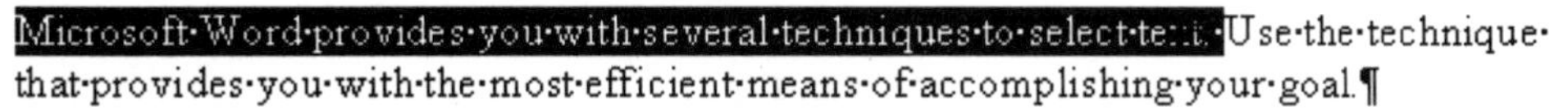

Microsoft·Word·provides·you·with·several·techniques·to·select·text.·Use·the·technique· that·provides·you·with·the·most·efficient·means·of·accomplishing·your·goal.¶

Figure 4-5   Selecting text.

Selecting Text

Selecting text is just a way to identify text on which you want to perform some procedure like adding text effects or removing it. Word provides you with several techniques to select text. Use the technique that provides you with the most efficient means of accomplishing your goal.

- Click and drag—This is the basic selection technique. Place your insertion point to the left of the text you want to select. Press and hold the left mouse button and drag through the text until all the characters have been highlighted.

- Double-click—Placing the mouse pointer over a word and double-clicking it selects that word.

- Triple-click—A triple click at a point in text selects an entire sentence.

- Line select—If you move your mouse pointer into the left margin, it changes to a right-pointing arrow. When you see that right-pointing arrow, clicking selects the adjacent line. You can drag through the following text to select multiple lines.

- Paragraph select—Double-clicking in the left margin selects the adjacent paragraph.

- Start and end point—This technique is useful for large areas of text, particularly text that runs to a second page or more. Place your insertion point to the left of the beginning character of the text you want to select. Without clicking your mouse, locate the end of the text block. Press and hold the Shift key and then click to the right of the final character. Release the mouse before you release the Shift key. All the text between your start and end points is selected.

- Entire document—To select the entire document, hold down the Ctrl key while pressing the A key.

NOTE   *Please be aware that when any text is selected it is replaced by the next keystroke. If you select your entire document and press the X key, for example, the entire document is replaced by the letter "x."*

Using Undo and Redo

The Undo and Redo buttons on the Standard toolbar comprise one of Word's most valuable features, as shown in Figure 4-6. If you have edited some text and then discover that it was the wrong text, by simply clicking the Undo button you can remove your edit. The Undo button reverses the last action you performed in Word. If you want to undo more than one action, click the drop-down arrow to the right of the Undo button and select the number of consecutive actions that you want to eliminate.

Figure 4-6   The Undo and Redo buttons from the Standard toolbar.

The Redo button restores actions reversed by the Undo button. Click it once, and the last undone action is restored. For multiple redos, click the drop-down arrow and select the consecutive actions you want to bring back. As you can imagine, this feature can be a real lifesaver at times.

NOTE   *Keep in mind one of the most effective text-editing techniques, cut, copy, and paste, which was discussed in "Skill 1: Use Common Office Tools." Remember, select the text, choose the Edit menu's Cut or Copy command, move to the new location, and choose the Edit menu's Paste command.*

Automatic Editing with AutoCorrect and AutoText

Two features of Word that are convenient and timesaving are AutoCorrect and AutoText. Both of these features may be considered editing techniques, but as they are quite remarkable and extremely useful, we are spotlighting them in their own section.

Using AutoCorrect

AutoCorrect automatically corrects typical misspellings and typos. Hundreds of typically mistyped words are already on AutoCorrect's list so that when you mistype a word on the list, AutoCorrect changes it immediately.

For example, if you type *taht*, intending to type *that*, AutoCorrect immediately changes the word to the correct spelling. If, for some reason, you want *taht* to remain, as we have in this paragraph, immediately click the Undo button on the Standard toolbar and the word is changed back.

Activating AutoCorrect

AutoCorrect is enabled by default when you first install Word. However, if it is not active, you can turn it on by following these steps:

1. **Open the AutoCorrect dialog box.**

   Choose the Tools menu's AutoCorrect Options command. Click the AutoCorrect tab, if necessary, as shown in Figure 4-7.

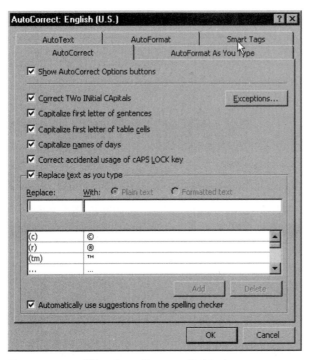

Figure 4-7   The AutoCorrect dialog box.

2. Select the Replace Text As You Type option.

The Replace Text As You Type option is located about midway down the AutoCorrect dialog box. Click to place a check mark in the check box and enable AutoCorrect.

3. Close the dialog box.

Click OK to save your changes to AutoCorrect and close the dialog box.

Adding New Words to the AutoCorrect List

New words can be added to the AutoCorrect list. For example, if you frequently type *manger* instead of *manager*, follow these steps to add it to the AutoCorrect list:

1. Open the AutoCorrect dialog box.

Choose the Tools menu's AutoCorrect Options command. Click the AutoCorrect tab, if necessary.

2. Enter the misspelling.

In the Replace box, type the word the way you frequently mistype it: *manger*.

3. **Enter the correct spelling.**

In the With box, type the word *manager* correctly.

4. **Add the word.**

Clicking the Add button places your word in the AutoCorrect list.

5. **Add other words if necessary.**

Add as many words as you like.

6. **Close the dialog box.**

Click OK to save your changes to the AutoCorrect word list and close the dialog box.

Deleting Words from the AutoCorrect List

To remove words from the AutoCorrect list, follow these steps:

1. **Open the AutoCorrect dialog box.**

Choose the Tools menu's AutoCorrect Options command. Click the AutoCorrect tab, if necessary.

2. **Select the word.**

Scroll through the AutoCorrect word list until you locate the word you want to remove, and click it.

3. **Delete the word.**

Clicking the Delete button permanently removes the word from the AutoCorrect list.

4. **Close the dialog box.**

Click OK to save your changes to the AutoCorrect list, and close the dialog box.

TIP *AutoCorrect can be used for tasks other than misspelled words. For example, if your organization's name is long and complicated, you can enter a code in the Replace box and type the full name in the With box. Then anytime you type the code, it is replaced by the full name of your organization. AutoCorrect's With box holds up to one paragraph of text.*

Using AutoText

Almost as much fun as AutoCorrect, AutoText is a Word feature that is particularly valuable to those who compile documents that use the same language over and over again. AutoText allows you to save text blocks of any size and easily insert them as needed.

Creating an AutoText Entry

For example, if you regularly generate contracts, some of which must contain a certain disclaimer, you can save the disclaimer language in AutoText and place it in the contracts with just a few keystrokes. To create the entry, follow these steps:

1. Type the text.

Enter the text in a new Word document, or locate the text in an existing file.

2. Select the text.

Select all the text that you want to save.

3. Open the AutoText dialog box.

AutoText is one of the tabs of the AutoCorrect dialog box. Choose the Tools menu's AutoCorrect Options command, and click the AutoText tab, as shown in Figure 4-8.

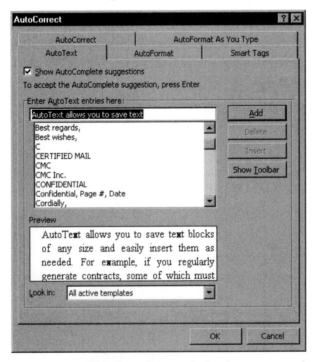

Figure 4-8   The AutoCorrect dialog box open to the AutoText tab.

4. **Name the text.**

Word enters the first few words of your text in the Enter AutoText Entries Here box. The text that appears in this box, however, acts as the name of the text entry and serves as a cue for placement of that text; therefore, you want it to be succinct. Replace the text that Word has provided with an easily recognizable name for the entry of five characters or more. Note the Preview box in the lower portion of the screen.

5. **Add the entry.**

Click the Add button to add your text to the text already in the program.

6. **Close the dialog box.**

Click OK to save your entry and close the dialog box.

Inserting an AutoText Entry

Now that the text has been placed in AutoText, it is available to use anytime you want. Follow these steps for insertion:

1. **Position your insertion point.**

Place your insertion point where you want the text to appear.

2. **Type the entry's name.**

After five or six characters have been typed, Word displays a small tag, called an AutoComplete Suggestion, displaying the remainder of the text's name.

3. **Accept the AutoComplete Suggestion.**

When you see the AutoComplete Suggestion, press the Enter key and the entire text is placed at the insertion point.

NOTE   *If you do not see the AutoComplete Suggestion, type in the name of the text entry and press the F3 key. The entry is placed in your document at the insertion point.*

Formatting Your Word Document

When you start Word, the resulting document is set with Margin, Orientation, Line Spacing, and Text Formatting defaults. Depending upon the particular usage you are making of the document and, more particularly, your own preferences, you may want to change some, or all, of those settings.

Formatting Text

You can change the way your document looks, quickly and easily, by changing the appearance of your type. And the easiest way to change that is through the use of the Formatting toolbar. All of the following techniques affect individual characters. Therefore, before making any of the changes discussed below, the text you want to format must be selected.

Changing the Type Face

Changing the typeface of your text is easily done. Select the text to be changed, and then click the drop-down arrow next to the Font box on the Formatting toolbar, as shown in Figure 4-9. Choose the new typeface from the list by clicking your choice. The selected text is changed to the new typeface.

Figure 4-9   The Font list from the Formatting toolbar.

Changing Type Size

Use the same technique to change type size as you used to change the typeface, above. First select the text to be changed, and then click the drop-down arrow beside the Font Size box, as shown in Figure 4-10. Select the point size you prefer.

Figure 4-10   The Font Size list from the Formatting toolbar.

Applying Font Effects

The use of bold, italicized, and underlined text can be used enhance your document and to emphasize main points. The Bold, Italics, and Underline buttons (B, I, and U buttons) on the Formatting toolbar, as shown in Figure 4-11, make this an easy task. Just select the text to which you want the text effect applied, and click the button of your choice.

Figure 4-11   The Bold, Italics, and Underline buttons from the Formatting toolbar.

To remove the formatting, select the affected text and click the button for the effect you want to remove.

NOTE   *More font effects are available in the Font dialog box. Select the text to be formatted, choose the Format menu's Font command, and then click the font effects of your choice. A sample of the effect on your type is shown in the Preview box at the bottom of the dialog box.*

Aligning Text

In Word, text alignment affects whole paragraphs and is selected from alignment buttons on the Formatting toolbar, as shown in Figure 4-12.

Figure 4-12   The Left, Center, Right, and Justified buttons from the Formatting toolbar.

- Left—This configuration aligns the text on the left but leaves a ragged (unaligned) right, as shown in Figure 4-13.

Left aligned text is the most common of
Word's four alignment choices. It aligns all
of the lines evenly on the left but not on the
right. This is called flush left, ragged right.

Figure 4-13   Left-aligned text.

- Center—As you would expect, this configuration centers the text between the two
  margins, leaving text to both the left and the right unaligned, as shown in Figure 4-14.

Center·aligned·text·is·just·that.·It·is·centered·
between·the·document's·margins.·In·this·
case,·both·the·left·side·and·the·right·side·of·
the·text·block·are·ragged.¶

Figure 4-14   Centered text.

- Right—Right-aligned text is even on the right and ragged on the left, as shown in
  Figure 4-15.

As you would expect, lines of right aligned
text are even to the right but ragged to the
left. This alignment style is the least used
of the four.

Figure 4-15   Right-aligned text.

- Justified—This configuration provides text that is aligned on both the left and the
  right, as shown in Figure 4-16.

Justified text is even on both the left and the
right. It is a traditional, more formal style
and is used for books, newspapers and even
business documents.

Figure 4-16   Justified text.

TIP   *Because text alignment in Word affects whole paragraphs, you do not need
to have a paragraph selected to establish its alignment. So long as your insertion point is in the paragraph, you can click any of the four alignment
buttons and your paragraph configures accordingly. If you want to align more
than one paragraph, select the paragraphs and then click a button to align
them all in one action.*

Setting Line Spacing

Line spacing can be set for the entire document or for a portion of it. If no text is selected when you change the Line Spacing settings, only the paragraph that contains the insertion point is altered. For multiple paragraphs or to change the entire document, select the text to be affected before altering the Line Spacing settings.

Choose the Format menu's Paragraph command to open the Paragraph dialog box. In the Spacing section, click the Line Spacing drop-down arrow, and make your choice of single, one-and-a-half, or double line spacing settings from the menu. If a more specific line spacing setting is desired, select At Least, Exactly, or Multiple from the Line Spacing box and select parameters from the At box to its right. Clicking OK closes the dialog box and applies your settings.

NOTE   *New to Office is the Line Spacing button on the Formatting toolbar, as shown in Figure 4-17. If you want to set your line spacing to conventional settings (1, 1.5, 2, 2.5, and 3 lines), the Line Spacing button is a quick fix. Merely click the drop-down arrow to the right of the button and make your selection. Keep in mind that the text you want to affect must be selected first.*

Figure 4-17   The Line Spacing button from the Formatting toolbar.

Inserting Page Breaks

Word automatically breaks text at the end of a page and starts it again at the beginning of the next page. However, if you want to break a page at a point other than that, choose the Insert menu's Break command and select the Page Break option. A page break is indicated by a dotted line with the words *Page Break* centered within it.

NOTE   *If your page break is shown visually as if one piece of paper ends and another follows just below it, you are viewing your document in the Print Layout view, which shows the document as it looks when printed. Either the Print Layout view or the Normal view may be used and are mostly a matter of preference. Make your selection from the View menu.*

Formatting Your Page Setup

Use the Page Setup dialog box, as shown in Figure 4-18, to set document structures such as margins and page orientation. To access the Page Setup dialog box, choose the File menu's Page Setup command.

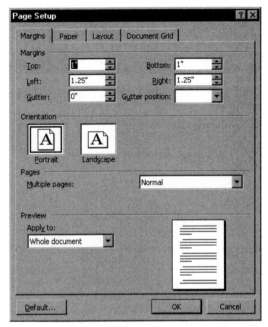

Figure 4-18 The Page Setup dialog box.

Setting Margins

Setting the margins determines how far the text is from the edges of the paper. You may want to change the margin settings to suit your own preference or for a particular type of document you create.

1. Open the Margins tab.

If the Margins tab is not open, click it to open it.

2. Enter the top margin setting.

In the Margins section, click the Top spin box to select the current setting. Then enter the distance you want from the top of the page to the first line of text in inches.

3. Tab to the Left spin box.

Pressing the Tab key moves the insertion point to the Left spin box and selects the current setting.

4. **Enter the left margin setting.**

Enter a margin setting.

5. **Repeat for the remaining two margin settings.**

Set the remaining two margins in the same manner, tabbing after each.

6. **Click OK.**

After all the margin settings have been entered, clicking OK applies the margins to your document. However, if you have other changes to make within the Page Setup dialog box, you may want to complete them before clicking OK.

Setting Document Orientation

Document orientation is the way the text is positioned on the page for reading. Portrait orientation means that the page is in a vertical position while being read, as in a standard business letter. Landscape puts the paper in a horizontal position, as shown in Figure 4-19. You might put a page in Landscape to accommodate wide tables or illustrations.

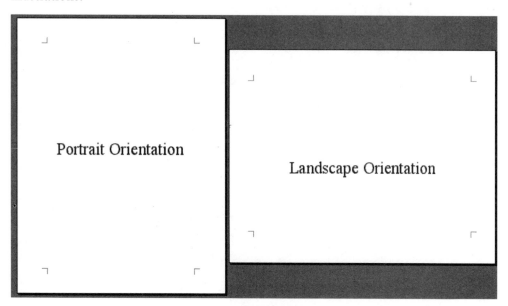

Figure 4-19   Portrait and Landscape orientations.

Portrait and Landscape orientation is selected on the Margins tab of the Page Setup dialog box. Click your preference, and then click OK to apply the orientation to your document.

Using Wizards

A wizard is an easy-to-use mini program built into Word that automatically performs a specific procedure for you. You just supply the parameters of the project in response to the wizard's questions and the wizard does the work.

The wizards available in Word include legal pleadings, memos, letters, faxes, reports, theses, directories, newsletters, manuals, brochures, calendars, Web pages, time sheets, agendas, résumés, purchase orders, and invoices. Access these wizards by choosing the File menu's New command and then clicking the General Templates link in the New Document pane. In addition to templates, this dialog box provides most of the wizards mentioned above. Just click the wizard's icon, and follow the directions specific to that project, as shown in Figure 4-20.

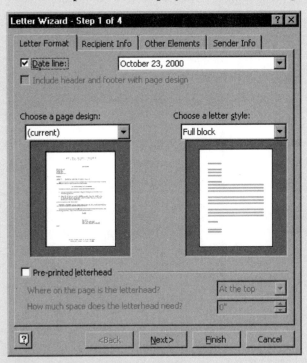

Figure 4-20 Word's Letter Wizard.

Spelling and Grammar Checking

Whether you are creating a business letter, a report, or a fax transmittal, the document you produce represents you. Because you want your documents to reflect on you positively, Word comes with powerful helpers that facilitate a document with correct spelling and good grammar. Although they are not foolproof (a lot depends upon you), using the Spelling Checker and the Grammar Checker greatly diminishes the chance of errors in your document. Whether you use the automated Check As You Type features or choose to use the traditional full-document check, you will find the Spelling and Grammar Checkers invaluable.

Checking Spelling and Grammar as You Type

By default, the Check Spelling As You Type and Check Grammar As You Type features are enabled. That means that Word works in the background to check every word, as you type it, and every sentence, as you finish it, for errors. If Word finds a possible spelling error (in other words, encounters a word not in its dictionary), the program indicates the possible error by underlining the word with a red wavy line. Likewise, possible grammar errors are indicated by a green wavy line.

When you encounter these indicators, place your mouse pointer over the word or words in question and right-click your mouse. A shortcut menu pops onto your screen offering you suggested corrections (if available). You can accept the suggested correction or tell the computer to ignore the error. The wavy line is removed from your document.

NOTE   *If you select Ignore, sometimes the wavy line returns. Although it may be a bit of a distraction, it does not print, so its being there is not a matter for concern.*

If the Check As You Type features are not active, choose the Tools menu's Options command and click the Spelling & Grammar tab. Click the Check Spelling As You Type and Check Grammar As You Type check boxes. Click OK to turn on the feature.

Running a Full-Document Spelling and Grammar Check

An alternative to the Check As You Type feature is the full-document Spelling And Grammar Checker. This tool can be opened by clicking the Spelling And Grammar button on the Standard toolbar, as shown in Figure 4-21.

Figure 4-21 The Spelling And Grammar button from the Standard toolbar.

In the Spelling And Grammar dialog box, as shown in Figure 4-22, the upper text box displays the possible spelling or grammar error while the lower box provides suggested corrections. You can respond to the error in any one of six ways by clicking the appropriate button.

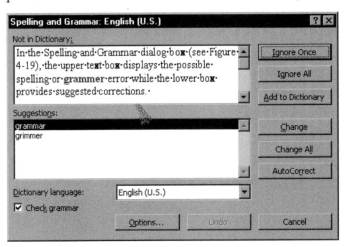

Figure 4-22 The Spelling And Grammar dialog box.

- Ignore Once—If you want to leave the text as it is, click the Ignore Once button. However, if the checker encounters the same configuration later in your document it still considers it a possible error.

- Ignore All—If you want to leave intact every instance of the identified text, click the Ignore All button. The Spelling And Grammar Checker ignores that configuration throughout the remainder of your document.

- Add To Dictionary—The checker lists any word that it does not find in the dictionary as a possible error. Therefore, you may want to add words, such as proper names or technical terminology that is used frequently, to the dictionary. Click the Add To Dictionary button and the Spelling Checker ignores that word from now on.

- Change—This option substitutes the selected suggestion for the possible error. However it changes only that one instance. If the checker encounters the same configuration later in the document it considers it a possible error again.

- Change All—When you want every instance of the possible error changed to the selected suggestion, click the Change All button. This affects the current document only.

- AutoCorrect—If you find that you are frequently mistyping or misspelling a word, you may want to add it to the AutoCorrect word list. And you can do it right in the Spelling And Grammar dialog box. Clicking the AutoCorrect button opens the AutoCorrect dialog box. You can then enter the word as described above.

NOTE   *It is important to understand that the Spelling Checker does not identify a misspelled word if the misspelling creates a word found in the Spelling dictionary. It is important that you proof your work.*

Using the Thesaurus

The Word Thesaurus is a handy feature to help you add variety and accuracy to your documents through the identification of synonyms and antonyms. The online Thesaurus works very much like the book form but may actually be easier to use. You can use the Thesaurus dialog box for in-depth word research or you can use the quick shortcut menu method.

The Thesaurus Dialog Box

Place your insertion point in the word you would like to look up. Then open the Thesaurus by choosing the Tools menu's Language command and choosing Thesaurus from the submenu.

The Thesaurus dialog box is composed of two columns, as shown in Figure 4-23. The left column shows the word that you have looked up followed by that word's various meanings. When you select a specific meaning in the left column, synonyms for that meaning appear in the right column.

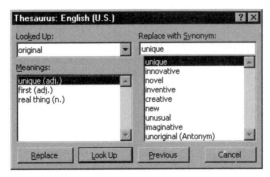

Figure 4-23 The Thesaurus dialog box.

You can also select any word in either column and then click the Look Up button to find the synonyms of that word. The word that you select in the right column replaces your looked-up word in your document when you click the Replace button.

The Shortcut Menu

The fastest way to find synonyms for a word is to use the shortcut menu. Position your mouse pointer over the word and right-click. When the shortcut menu pops up, choose the Synonyms command, as shown in Figure 4-24. Clicking one of the words in the submenu tells Word to replace the original word with the one you selected.

Figure 4-24 The shortcut menu and Synonyms submenu.

TIP   *Note that you can access the Thesaurus dialog box by choosing the Thesaurus command from the submenu. If you do not want to substitute any of the words on the submenu for your word, press the Esc key twice. The submenu and the shortcut menu disappear.*

Skill 5

USE EXCEL FOR SPREADSHEET FUNCTIONS

Featuring:

- Anatomy of a Workbook
- Moving Around a Workbook
- Entering Data
- Formatting Data and Worksheets
- Inserting and Deleting Cells, Rows, Columns, and Worksheets
- Copying, Cutting, and Pasting
- Charting Your Work

Before computerized spreadsheet programs, financial and accounting spreadsheets were created by hand with a lot of care, time, and tedium. Workbooks were (usually) massive covers with multiple sheets for multiple usages. Today, it is all so much easier. Microsoft Excel is a powerful business tool for any job that requires the compilation, processing, and analysis of data.

Anatomy of a Workbook

When you start Excel, it automatically opens an empty workbook file called Book1. In reality, an Excel workbook is not too different from the old massive binder and multiple sheets. It is far easier to handle and does all the math for you, but it looks somewhat the same.

Worksheets

A worksheet is very much like a page from the old-fashioned binder. It is made up of columns and rows but holds far more data than a columnar page ever did. By default, new Excel workbooks open with three worksheets, indicated by the sheet tabs at the bottom of the screen. However, spreadsheets may be added to a maximum of 256 and may be deleted until there is only one. The Excel spreadsheet appears in the area between the formula bar and the status bar.

Columns

In a spreadsheet, columns, which run vertically through the length of the sheet, are indicated by letters of the alphabet. Each spreadsheet in a workbook contains 256 columns.

Rows

Numbers identify rows, which run horizontally through the width of the spreadsheet. There are 65,536 rows in each spreadsheet.

Cells

The intersection of a column and row is called a cell. Each cell has an address, called a reference, consisting of the column letter and row number. For example, the cell in the top left corner of the worksheet is cell A1.

A dark outline called the cell selector identifies the active cell. Figure 5-1 shows the cell selector in cell C8. If you type a number and press the Enter key, Excel places the number in the active cell.

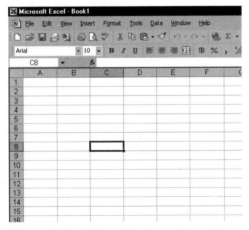

Figure 5-1   The cell selector identifies cell C8 as the active cell.

Name Box

The reference of the active cell appears in the Name box, which is on the left side of the line immediately above the column indicators.

Formula Bar

On the same line as the Name box is the formula bar. The formula bar displays the data you enter in your worksheet.

Moving Around a Workbook

With three (or more) sheets, 256 columns, and 65,536 rows, an Excel workbook is so large that only a small area is visible onscreen at one time. Not surprisingly, Excel provides several ways for you to view different portions of the workbook displayed in the program window:

- With the mouse, you can use the vertical and horizontal scroll bars along the right and bottom edges of the document window to move through your worksheet. Just click inside the scroll bars to move one screen at a time. Click the scroll bar arrows to move one row or column.

- With the mouse, click a sheet tab to move to that worksheet in the workbook.

- The standard navigation keys, Page Up and Page Down, move through your worksheet one screen at a time. When you hold down the Ctrl key and press Page Up or Page Down, you move to the previous or next worksheet.

- The arrow keys move up and down, right and left one cell at a time. You can also move to the right one cell by pressing the Tab key and to the left one cell by holding down the Shift key while pressing Tab.

TIP   *To move directly to a specific cell, you can enter that cell's reference in the Name box and press the Enter key. You can also choose the Edit menu's Go To command. When you choose this command, Excel displays the Go To dialog box. You can enter a cell reference in its Reference text box and then click OK to move to the cell.*

Entering Data

Excel worksheets can contain four kinds of data: labels, values, formulas, and functions.

NOTE   *While functions are really a type of formula, they have a specific format and usage. Therefore, we are discussing them independently.*

Entering Labels

Labels are simply any information entered in a worksheet that you don't want to manipulate arithmetically. They often identify the values that are subject to calculation, so you normally enter them as the first stage in setting up a worksheet. Usually, labels are pieces of text, such as the expense categories in a budgeting worksheet or the employee names in a payroll worksheet. However, they can also be numbers that won't be used arithmetically, such as telephone numbers or part or project ID numbers.

To enter a label, follow these steps:

1. Move the cell selector to the desired location.

You can do this by clicking the cell, using the navigation keys to move the cell selector, or using the Name box.

2. Type the label.

As you do, Excel displays what you type in the formula bar. It also adds the Enter button (the one that looks like a check mark) and the Cancel button (the one that looks like an X) to the formula bar.

3. Set the label in the cell.

You can do this by pressing the Enter key, clicking the Enter button on the formula bar, or moving to another cell.

Figure 5-2 shows a simple workbook fragment with just a handful of labels. Notice that Excel aligns text to the left edge of each cell and allows long labels to spill over into adjacent cells if they are unoccupied.

	A	B	C	D	E	F	G
1	Budget 2002						
2			January	February	March	Totals	Averages
3	Mortgage						
4	Power						
5	Telephone						
6	Transportation						
7	Insurance						
8	Recreation						
9							
10							

Figure 5-2   A worksheet with labels entered.

Entering Values

Values are numbers you want to add, subtract, multiply, divide, or otherwise manipulate in formulas. In a budgeting worksheet, for example, you would enter the budgeted amounts as values. Figure 5-3 shows the values, or amounts, entered beside each of the worksheet labels.

	A	B	C	D	E	F	G
1	Budget 2002						
2			January	February	March	Totals	Averages
3	Mortgage		1000	1000	1000		
4	Power		235	235	175		
5	Telephone		75	75	75		
6	Transportation		375	375	375		
7	Insurance		895				
8	Recreation		2500	200	1500		

Figure 5-3   A budgeting worksheet with labels and values.

To enter values, use the 10 number keys either on the main keyboard or on the numeric keypad. To use the numeric keypad, the Num Lock key must be selected. Use the period key to show decimal places and the hyphen key to identify negative values.

To enter values, use the same three-step process as you do to enter labels. For example, to enter the value *1000* shown in cell C3, follow these steps:

1. Move the cell selector to the desired cell.

In Figure 5-3, for example, you move the cell selector to C3 to enter the first value. You do this by clicking in cell C3.

2. Type the value.

As you do, Excel displays the number in the formula bar. It also adds the Enter and Cancel buttons to the formula bar.

3. Set the value in the cell.

As with setting a label, you can do this by pressing the Enter key, clicking the Enter button on the formula bar, or moving to another cell.

To enter the rest of the values shown in Figure 5-3, repeat the steps above for each value.

Entering Formulas

Excel's power stems from its ability to perform calculations on the values you have stored in a workbook—something you do with formulas and functions. Excel calculates formulas automatically. You enter them in a worksheet cell in the same way as you do with labels and values. In the cell, however, Excel displays not the formula, but its result. For example, if you enter a formula that says to add 4 and 2, Excel retains the formula and displays it in the formula bar when the cell is selected, but Excel displays the result, 6, in the worksheet itself.

Formula Fundamentals

Formulas must begin with the equal sign (=); that is how Excel distinguishes them from values and labels. You can construct formulas that subtract, multiply, divide, and exponentiate. The – symbol means subtraction, the * means multiplication, the / means division, and the ^ means exponential operation. Table 5-1 shows the different mathematical operators and the results they return.

FORMULA ENTERED	RESULT DISPLAYED IN CELL
=4+2	6
=4-2	2
=4*2	8
=4/2	2
=4^2	16

Table 5-1   A list of simple formulas illustrating the standard arithmetic operators.

Figure 5-4 shows a simple budgeting worksheet built from Figure 5-3. The formula used in cell C9 appears in the formula bar and the result is displayed in the worksheet.

Figure 5-4   A budgeting worksheet with a formula entered and the result displayed.

To build more complicated formulas, you need to recognize the standard rules of operator precedence: Excel first performs exponential operations, then multiplication and division operations, and finally, addition and subtraction.

For example, in the equation =1+2*3^4, Excel first raises 3 to the fourth power to get 81. It then multiplies this value by 2 to get 162. Finally, it adds 1 to this value to get 163.

To override these rules, you must use parentheses. You can use multiple sets of parentheses in a formula as need be. Excel first performs the function in the innermost set of parentheses. Take the following formulas in Table 5-2 as an example:

Formula entered	Result displayed in cell
=1+2*3^4	163
=(1+2)*3^4	243
=((1+2)*3)^4	6561

Table 5-2   A list of formulas that show how parentheses override operator procedure.

Using Cell References

In the budgeting worksheet, you could total the budgeted expenses by entering the formula =1000+235+75+375+895+2500 in cell C9. There is, however, a practical problem with this approach: You would need to rewrite the formula each time any of the values changed. Because this approach is unwieldy, Excel also allows you to use cell references in formulas. When a formula includes a cell reference, Excel uses the value that cell contains. For example, to add the budgeted amounts on your budgeting worksheet using a formula with cell references, follow these steps:

1. Move the cell selector to C9.

You can do this by clicking cell C9. Or you can use the arrow keys.

2. Type =C3+C4+C5+C6+C7+C8.

If you make a mistake entering this formula, you can edit it in the same way that you edit any label or value.

3. Press the Enter key, or click the Enter button.

Excel enters your formula in the cell, calculates the formula, and then displays the formula result, as shown in Figure 5-5.

C9	▼	f_x =C3+C4+C5+C6+C7+C8				
	A	B	C	D	E	F	G
1			Budget 2002				
2			January	February	March	Totals	Averages
3	Mortgage		1000	1000	1000		
4	Power		235	235	235		
5	Telephone		75	75	75		
6	Transportation		375	375	375		
7	Insurance		895	0	0		
8	Recreation		2500	200	1500		
9	Totals		5080	1885	3185		

Figure 5-5   A worksheet with cell references used in a formula.

To reference a cell on the same worksheet as the formula, you need to supply only the column-letter-and-row-number cell reference. To reference cell C3 on the same worksheet, for example, you enter *C3*.

You can also reference cells on other worksheets. To reference a cell on another worksheet in the same workbook, however, you need to precede the cell reference with the name of the worksheet and an exclamation point symbol. To reference cell C1 on the worksheet named Sheet2, for example, you enter *Sheet2!C1*.

You can reference cells in other workbooks, too. To do this most easily, open the other workbooks, begin building your formula as described earlier in this skill, and then click the other workbook cell you want to reference at the point you want to include the reference. Excel then writes the full cell reference for you, which includes the workbook name. An external reference to cell C3 on the worksheet named Sheet2 in the workbook named Budget might be written as =[Budget.xls]Sheet2!C3.

Understanding Worksheet Recalculation

As you build and edit your worksheet, Excel automatically updates the formulas and recalculates their results. For example, in the budgeting worksheet, if you change the value in cell C3 from 1000 to 1500, Excel recalculates any formulas that use the value stored in cell C3. As a result, the formula in cell C9 returns the value 3400—an increase of five hundred.

In simple worksheets such as the one shown in Figure 5-5, recalculation takes place so quickly you won't even be aware it is occurring. In larger worksheets with hundreds or even thousands of formulas, however, recalculation is much slower. The mouse pointer changes to the hourglass symbol when Excel is busy recalculating.

If you don't want Excel to automatically recalculate formulas as you are working, choose the Tools menu's Options command and click the Calculation tab. Then click the Manual option button under Calculation, and click OK. The word *Calculate* appears on the status bar when your worksheet needs to be recalculated. You can force recalculation by pressing the F9 key.

Formula Errors

It is possible to build an illogical or unsolvable formula. When you do, Excel displays an error message in the cell rather than calculating the result. The error message, which begins with the # symbol, describes the error. Suppose, for example, that you enter the formula =1/0 in a cell. Because division by zero is an undefined mathematical operation, Excel can't solve the formula. To alert you to this, Excel displays the error message #DIV/0!.

Another common error is a circular reference. This occurs when two or more formulas indirectly depend on one another to achieve a result. For example, if the formula in cell A1 is =A2 and the formula in cell A2 is =A1+A3+A4, A1 depends on A2 and A2 depends on A1. Excel displays a warning and the Circular Reference toolbar when you create a circular reference. Excel identifies circular references by displaying the word *Circular* on the status bar and showing the address of the cell whose formula completed the "circle." It also draws arrows between the cells causing the circle.

To fix a formula error, edit the erroneous formula using the same techniques as with label and value editing. Move the cell selector to the cell holding the formula, click the formula bar, and edit the formula. When the formula is correct, set it by moving the cell selector, pressing the Enter key, or clicking the Enter button.

NOTE   *When a formula refers to a cell that contains an erroneous formula, both formulas return the error message. For example, if cell A1 attempts to divide by zero and cell A2 refers to cell A1, cell A2 returns the error message #DIV/ 0! as well.*

Functions

Excel provides several hundred prebuilt formulas, called functions, that provide a shortcut to constructing complicated or lengthy formulas. In general, a function accepts input values, or arguments, and then makes some calculation and returns a result.

Excel provides financial, statistical, mathematical, trigonometric, and even engineering functions. Each function has a name that describes its operation. The function that adds values is named SUM, for example, and the function that calculates an arithmetic mean, or average, is named AVERAGE.

Most functions require arguments, or input values, which you enclose in parentheses. The ROUND function, for example, rounds a specific value to a specified number of decimal places. To round the value 5.75 to the nearest tenth, you could use the function shown below:

=ROUND(5.75, 1)

Even if a function doesn't require arguments, you still need to include the parentheses. For example, the function PI returns the mathematical constant pi. The function needs no arguments, but you still need to enter it as =PI().

Functions can use values, formulas, and even other functions as arguments. If entered in the budgeting worksheet shown in Figure 5-5, for example, each of the following functions returns the same result, 5080:

=SUM(C3:C8)

=SUM(C3,C4,C5,C6,C7,C8)

=SUM(1000,235,75,375,895,2500)

=SUM(SUM(C3),SUM(C4),SUM(C5),SUM(C6),SUM(C7),SUM(C8))

NOTE   *Because summing is such a common spreadsheet operation, Excel provides an AutoSum button on the toolbar; you can use it to enter an =SUM function in the active cell of a contiguous range of cells. If cell C9 in the worksheet shown in Figure 5-5 were empty, for example, and you selected the range C3:C8, you could click the AutoSum toolbar button to direct Excel to place the formula =SUM(C3:C8) in cell C9.*

TIP   *To identify a toolbar button, point to the button. Excel displays the button name in a small box called a ToolTip. If you point to the button that shows the Greek sigma character, for example, Excel displays a ToolTip box identifying the button as the AutoSum button.*

To most easily insert complicated functions and reduce your chance of error, click the Insert Function button to the left of the formula bar (identified by *fx*) or choose the Insert menu's Function command. This displays the Insert Function dialog box, as shown in Figure 5-6. Type a brief description of what you want to do in the box provided, or select a category from the drop-down list box. Because some of the functions are a little difficult to recognize or distinguish by name, Excel describes what the selected function does at the bottom of the Insert Function dialog box. After you have found the function you want to use, click OK.

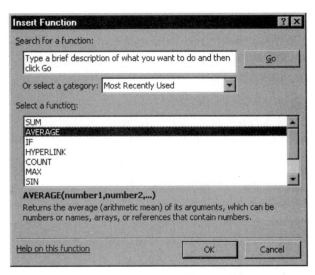

Figure 5-6   The Insert Function dialog box.

Excel displays the second Insert Function dialog box with text boxes you can use to identify or supply the arguments required for the function, as shown in Figure 5-7. If you know the cell reference or the range you need for the argument, type it in the appropriate argument box.

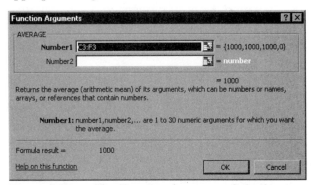

Figure 5-7   The Function Arguments dialog box.

However, if you need to look back at your spreadsheet, Excel provides a convenient way to do so. To the right of each argument box there is a Collapse/Expand button that allows you to temporarily collapse the dialog box, leaving just the argument box showing, as shown in Figure 5-8. This provides access to the data. (You can drag the argument box to another location on your screen, if necessary.) Click the cell or drag through the appropriate range and the data is entered in the argument box. Then click the button to the right of the argument box to expand the dialog box back to your screen. Do the same for any other arguments that may be required by the function. Click OK when you are finished. Excel pastes the function in the cell.

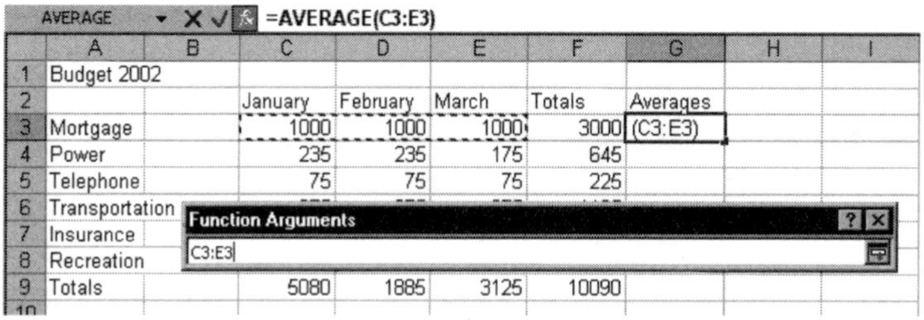

Figure 5-8   Selecting data required for a function.

NOTE   *A range is simply any group of cells of the worksheet. It can consist of only two cells or several hundred. Excel uses opposite corner cell references and a colon to define ranges. For example, the range of cells from C1 and up to and including C5 is written as C1:C5. And the range of cells from C1 to D2 is written as C1:D2.*

You will need to repeat the process for each formula or function needed to complete your worksheet, as shown in Figure 5-9. Although functions shorten the time it would take to think through and write out complicated formulas, re-creating functions or formulas over and over again can be time consuming, particularly in a very large worksheet. In the section on "Copying, Cutting, and Pasting," later in this skill, you will learn how to repeat functions and formulas quickly and easily.

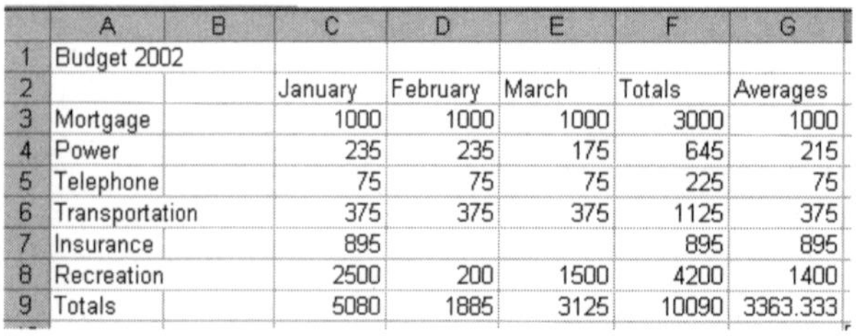

Figure 5-9   The completed budgeting worksheet.

Formatting Data and Worksheets

When you first enter data in a worksheet, it is unformatted. Labels are entered in the default font and font size (Arial, 10 pt), and values are shown without commas, currency symbols, or even decimal places, unless you enter decimal places with the data. This leaves the appropriate formatting up to you.

This section describes many of the ways in which you may alter the appearance, and even the structure, of a worksheet.

Aligning Labels and Values

Excel normally aligns numbers against the right edge of a cell and text against the left edge. You can override these default alignments by using the Left Align, Center, Right Align, and Merge And Center buttons on the Formatting toolbar.

The Left Align, Center, and Right Align toolbar buttons work as you might expect. For example, to left-align the contents of selected cells, click the Left Align button.

The Merge And Center toolbar button is a little more complex. It lets you center a label across a selection of cells. For example, you can enter a label in cell A1 of the budgeting worksheet and then center it across the range A1:G1. To do so, first select the range and then click the Merge And Center toolbar button. Figure 5-10 shows the worksheet after this alignment.

A1		f_x	Budget 2002				
	A	B	C	D	E	F	G
1				Budget 2002			
2			January	February	March	Totals	Averages
3	Mortgage		1000	1000	1000	3000	1000
4	Power		235	235	175	645	215
5	Telephone		75	75	75	225	75
6	Transportation		375	375	375	1125	375
7	Insurance		895			895	895
8	Recreation		2500	200	1500	4200	1400
9	Totals		5080	1885	3125	10090	3363.333

Figure 5-10   A label centered across the range A1:G1.

Formatting Numbers

You can assign numeric formats such as dollar signs, percentage symbols, and commas. To quickly assign these specific, common formats, select the cell or range you want to format and click the Currency Style, Percent Style, or Comma Style buttons on the Formatting toolbar, as shown in Figure 5-11.

Figure 5-11 The Currency Style, Percent Style, and Comma Style buttons from the Standard toolbar.

Using the Format Cells Command

You can access a more sophisticated array of formatting features by selecting the cell or range you want to format, choosing the Format menu's Cells command, and clicking the appropriate tab.

In the Alignment tab, the Horizontal drop-down list box lets you align cell contents in the same ways as the Left Align, Center, Right Align, and Merge And Center buttons do as shown in Figure 5-12. The Vertical drop-down list box allows you to align cell contents at the top, center, or bottom of the cell. The Orientation box allows you to rotate the cell contents.

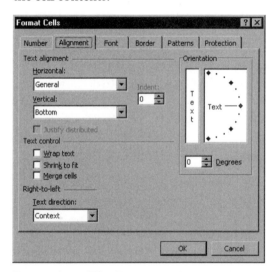

Figure 5-12 The Format Cells dialog box open at the Alignment tab.

The Text Control check boxes provide you with several more specialized alignment options. The Wrap Text check box allows you to wrap a long line of text into multiple lines in a single cell. The number of lines varies depending on the amount of text and the width of the cell. The Shrink To Fit check box allows you to decrease the size of the numbers or letters in a cell so that they fit in the current size constraints of the cell. The Merge Cells check box allows you to combine cells into larger, single cells.

To assign numeric formats other than those on the Formatting toolbar, follow these steps:

1. Open the Number tab of the Format Cells dialog box.

Choose the Format menu's Cells command, and click the Number tab of the Format Cells dialog box, as shown in Figure 5-13.

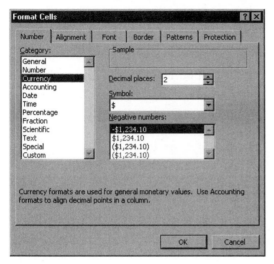

Figure 5-13 The Format Cells dialog box open to the Number tab.

2. Select a numeric formatting category from the Category list box.

In a budgeting worksheet, you would probably choose the Accounting category.

3. Use the boxes and buttons for the category you chose to specify the exact formatting.

In a budgeting worksheet, for example, you might need to select a different currency symbol from the Symbol drop-down list box.

4. Click OK.

Changing Font and Font Size

Excel offers a wide variety of choices for changing a selected font's appearance, such as by adding boldfacing or underlining, for changing a font, and for specifying a different size.

To add effects such as boldfacing, italics, and underlining, you can use the Bold, Italic, and Underline font buttons on the Formatting toolbar. To use any of these buttons, simply select the worksheet range you want to format and then click the button.

NOTE   *If you are creating an Excel worksheet that you intend to publish on the World Wide Web, you probably don't want to use underlines in your formatting. Underlines are usually reserved for hyperlinks.*

To change the font of text, click the down-arrow beside the Font toolbar button and select a font from the list. If you open the Font drop-down list box, Excel displays the font's name using the font itself, so you can preview it, as shown in Figure 5-14. Fonts listed with a TT icon beside them are TrueType fonts. Fonts built into your printer have a printer icon next to them. If you use a TrueType font, the font you see on your screen will be the same one that the printer prints. If you use a scalable printer font and the printer you use doesn't support your selection, the printer uses the closest-matching font.

Figure 5-14   The Font drop-down list box.

To change the size of text, click the down arrow beside the Size toolbar button. Fonts are measured using points. One point is 1/72 of an inch. So a point size of 18 means that the font is ¼ inch tall. Excel's default point size is 10. You probably don't want to use fonts smaller than 10 points for legibility.

Modifying Column and Row Size

As you reformat the labels and values in your worksheet, you may need to modify the standard column and row sizes to accommodate your formatting changes. To quickly increase the column width to accommodate all text in the column but include no extra white space, double-click the right border of that column heading. Normally, Excel automatically increases row height when you increase point size, but you can perform the same trick on rows by double-clicking the lower border of a row heading. This expands the row to the smallest height possible that still fits all entries within that row.

To specify exact column width, select any cell in that column, choose the Format menu's Column command and then choose Width from the submenu. Enter the width in characters in the Column Width text box, as shown in Figure 5-15, and click OK.

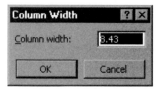

Figure 5-15 The Column Width text box.

To specify exact row height, select any cell in that row, choose the Format menu's Row command, and then choose Height from the submenu. Enter the height in points in the Row Height text box, and click OK.

To hide a row, select any cell in the row, choose the Format menu's Row command, and then choose Hide from the submenu. To redisplay a hidden row, select a range that includes cells in the rows above and below the hidden row. Then choose the Format menu's Row command, and choose Unhide from the submenu.

To hide a column, select any cell in the column, choose the Format menu's Column command, and then choose Hide from the submenu. To redisplay a hidden column, select a range that includes cells in the columns to the left and right of the hidden column. Then choose the Format menu's Column command, and choose Unhide from the submenu.

Excel attempts to adjust the cell references and range definitions used in formulas for row and column insertions and deletions. For example, if a formula uses values in column C and you delete column B so that column C becomes the new column B, Excel adjusts the formulas to read column B. If you delete a cell referenced in a formula, however, Excel replaces the formula's reference with the error message #REF, indicating that the formula originally referenced a now-deleted cell.

Using AutoFormat

Excel's AutoFormat feature performs many standard formatting tasks in a single operation: setting fonts, aligning labels, setting column width and row height, establishing numeric and date/time formats, and adding borders and rules.

To use AutoFormat, you first enter worksheet labels, values, and formulas, as shown in Figure 5-16.

	A	B	C	D	E	F	G
1				Budget 2002			
2			January	February	March	Totals	Averages
3	Mortgage		1000	1000	1000	3000	1000
4	Power		235	235	175	645	215
5	Telephone		75	75	75	225	75
6	Transportation		375	375	375	1125	375
7	Insurance		895			895	895
8	Recreation		2500	200	1500	4200	1400
9	Totals		5080	1885	3125	10090	3363.333

Figure 5-16 The budgeting worksheet before an AutoFormat is applied.

To use the AutoFormat command, follow these steps:

1. Select the worksheet range you want to format.

In Figure 5-16, you would select the range A1:G9.

2. Open the AutoFormat dialog box.

Choose the Format menu's AutoFormat command, as shown in Figure 5-17.

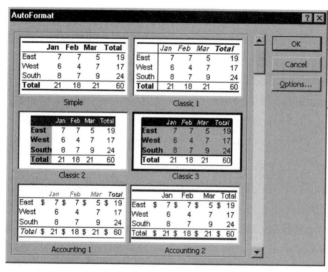

Figure 5-17 The AutoFormat dialog box.

3. Select the AutoFormatting options you want to use.

Click the Options button if you want to specify which AutoFormatting options should be applied to your worksheet selection. When you do this, Excel adds Options check boxes to the AutoFormat dialog box. Select and clear these check boxes to selectively apply individual components of an AutoFormat.

4. Select an AutoFormat by clicking it.

The AutoFormat pictures show roughly what the AutoFormat formatting looks like.

5. Click OK to apply the format to the range you selected.

Figure 5-18 shows what the budgeting worksheet looks like after the AutoFormat selected in Figure 5-17 is applied.

	A	B	C	D	E	F	G
1				Budget 2002			
2			January	February	March	Totals	Averages
3	Mortgage		1000	1000	1000	3000	1000
4	Power		235	235	175	645	215
5	Telephone		75	75	75	225	75
6	Transportation		375	375	375	1125	375
7	Insurance		895			895	895
8	Recreation		2500	200	1500	4200	1400
9	Totals		5080	1885	3125	10090	3363.333333

Figure 5-18   A worksheet range with an AutoFormat applied.

Inserting and Deleting Cells, Rows, Columns, and Worksheets

Excel lets you insert and delete cells, rows, columns, and worksheets in your workbook with speed and efficiency. You can easily delete what you no longer need or insert new items between existing entries when you need more space.

Using the Insert Command

To insert a row, click any cell in the row below where you want a row inserted. Then choose the Insert menu's Rows command.

To insert a column, click any cell in the column to the right of where you want a column inserted and choose the Insert menu's Columns command.

To insert a cell in a column or row, right-click the cell where you want the new cell to appear. Excel displays the Insert dialog box, as shown in Figure 5-19. Click the Shift Cells Right button to insert a new cell in a row or click the Shift Cells Down button to insert a new cell in a column. After you have selected the appropriate option button, click OK.

Figure 5-19   The Insert dialog box.

To insert a worksheet, display the worksheet tab in front of which you want to create a new worksheet and choose the Insert menu's Worksheet command.

Using the Delete Command

To delete a cell, range, row, or column, select the specific cell or range or any cell in the row or column you want to delete and choose the Edit menu's Delete command. Excel displays the Delete dialog box, as shown in Figure 5-20. Describe whether you want to shift the remaining cells up or to the left, or whether you want to delete the entire row or column, and click OK.

Figure 5-20 The Delete dialog box.

Naming Cells and Cell Ranges

In a small worksheet it is not too difficult to remember that cell C3 contains January's mortgage expense, C6 contains transportation costs, and so on. In the real world, however, Excel worksheets can be much more complex, and keeping track of what each cell represents becomes correspondingly more difficult. In this way, instead of referring to cell C3 in a formula, you could refer to JanMortgage if you first name the individual cell. For example, if you named cells C3, C4, C5, C6, C7, and C8 JanMortgage, JanPower, JanTelephone, JanTransportation, JanInsurance, and JanRecreation respectively, the following two formulas would be identical:

=C3+C4+C5+C6+C5+C8

=JanMortgage+JanPower+JanTelephone+JanTransportation+JanInsurance+JanRecreation

To name a cell or range, select the cell or range of cells to be named and then type the cell or range name in the Name box.

Copying, Cutting, and Pasting

You can copy or cut the contents of cells and ranges and then paste them into other locations. This means you don't have to repeatedly type a label, value, or formula. You can type the entry just once and then copy or move it.

TIP *With most programs, when you copy or cut something, the program places it on the Windows Clipboard. The only catch with the Windows Clipboard is that it can hold only one copied or cut piece of information at a time. So if you copy or cut another piece of information, the program replaces what the Clipboard previously stored. Office programs like Excel provide a nifty new feature called the Clipboard toolbar that allows you to store up to 24 pieces of copied or cut information at a time. To use the Clipboard toolbar, choose the View menu's Toolbars command and then choose Clipboard from the submenu.*

Copying Labels and Values

Suppose, for example, that the numbers shown in the first four rows of column C of the budgeting worksheet represent the unchanging budgeted expenses for January, February, and March, as shown in Figure 5-21. Rather than reenter the same values, you could copy the values already stored in column C.

	A	B	C	D	E
1			Budget 2002		
2			January	February	March
3	Mortgage		1000		
4	Power		235		
5	Telephone		75		
6	Transportation		375		
7	Insurance		895	0	0
8	Recreation		2500	200	1500
9	Totals		5080		

Figure 5-21 The simple budgeting worksheet.

To copy the labels and values for such an operation, follow these steps:

1. Select the cell or range to be copied.

In Figure 5-21, this would mean you select the range C3:C6. The easiest method for selecting a specific cell or range is by clicking or clicking and dragging the mouse.

2. Click the Copy toolbar button, or choose the Edit menu's Copy command.

When you do this, Excel places a copy of the labels and values on the Clipboard and indicates the copied cells with a scrolling marquee.

NOTE   *The scrolling marquee will remain around the range until you remove it or place another range on the Clipboard. To remove the scrolling marquee, press the Esc button.*

3. Select the destination cell or the cell in the upper left corner of the destination range.

If you want to duplicate the selected cells more than once, select the multiple destination ranges in their entirety. For the worksheet shown in Figure 5-21, for example, you would select the range D3:E6.

NOTE   *If you paste a copy of a single cell into a multiple-cell range, the contents of the cell are duplicated in each cell in the destination range.*

4. Click the Paste toolbar button, or choose the Edit menu's Paste command.

When you do this, Excel copies the worksheet range from the Clipboard into the specified worksheet range, as shown in Figure 5-22.

	A	B	C	D	E
1			Budget 2002		
2			January	February	March
3	Mortgage		1000	1000	1000
4	Power		235	235	235
5	Telephone		75	75	75
6	Transportation		375	375	375
7	Insurance		895	0	0
8	Recreation		2500	200	1500
9	Totals		5080		

Figure 5-22 A worksheet with two copies of C3:C6 pasted in D3:E6.

TIP   *You can also copy a cell or range with the mouse. Just select the cell or range, hold down the Ctrl key, point to the black border around the cell or range so that the mouse pointer changes from a cross to an arrow, and then drag the cell or range to a new location.*

Copying Formulas

When you copy labels and values, Excel duplicates the contents of the copied cell or cells and pastes the data into the selected range. When you copy a formula, however, Excel adjusts any cell references used in the formula. This important difference can be illustrated by copying the formula in cell C9 of Figure 5-22, =C1+C2+C3+C4+C5, into cells D9 and E9. To do this, follow these steps:

1. **Select the cell or range with the formula(s) you want to copy.**

   In the example of the worksheet shown in Figure 5-22, you would select cell C9.

2. **Click the Copy toolbar button.**

   Excel moves a copy of the formula in cell C9 to the Clipboard.

3. **Select the destination range D9:E9.**

   In the example of the worksheet shown in Figure 5-22, you would select the range D9:E9.

4. **Click the Paste toolbar button.**

   Excel adjusts the formulas for the column in question and pastes the formula =D3+D4+D5+D6+D7+D8 into cell D9 and the formula =E3+E4+E5+E6+E7+D8 into cell E9. Figure 5-23 shows the worksheet after copying the formula.

	A	B	C	D	E
1			Budget 2002		
2			January	February	March
3	Mortgage		1000	1000	1000
4	Power		235	235	235
5	Telephone		75	75	75
6	Transportation		375	375	375
7	Insurance		895	0	0
8	Recreation		2500	200	1500
9	Totals		5080	1885	3185

Figure 5-23 The budgeting worksheet after copying the formula in cell C9 into cells D9 and E9.

The formula changes that Excel makes aren't a mistake. Excel assumes—unless you tell it otherwise—that the cell references in your formulas are *relative*. When Excel copies and pastes a formula with relative cell references, it adjusts them.

To prevent Excel from automatically adjusting the relative references of copied formulas, you can make them *absolute*. Simply place a dollar sign ($) in front of the part or parts you don't want Excel to adjust. For example, to tell Excel not to adjust the formula at all, place a dollar sign in front of both the column letter and row number, like this: A1. To allow Excel to adjust row numbers but not column letters, put a dollar sign in front of the column letter but not the row number, like this: $A1. And to allow Excel to adjust column letters but not row numbers, put a dollar sign in front of the row number but not the column letter, like this: A$1.

Special Pasting Options

If you want to specify pasting options, instead of just clicking the Paste toolbar button after copying or cutting, choose the Edit menu's Paste Special command. Excel displays the Paste Special dialog box, as shown in Figure 5-24. To paste a row of cells as a column of cells or vice versa, select the Transpose check box. To paste only a portion of the copied or cut cells' contents, click a Paste option button other than All. For example, to paste only the comments in a cell, click the Comments option button in the Paste section. To add, subtract, multiply, or divide the values in the copied range with the values in the destination range, click the Add, Subtract, Multiply, or Divide option button in the Operation section. To tell Excel it shouldn't paste blank cells over values, select the Skip Blanks check box.

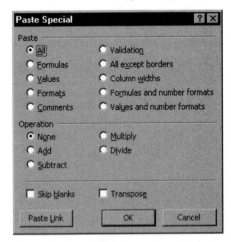

Figure 5-24 The Paste Special dialog box.

Moving Labels, Values, and Formulas

To move, rather than copy, a selected range, follow the same procedure, but click the Cut toolbar button or choose the Edit menu's Cut command instead of choosing the Copy command. Excel removes the selected contents from their original location and allows you to paste them in a new location.

NOTE   *When you move a formula, Excel doesn't adjust the relative references used in the moved formula.*

You can also move a cell or range with the mouse by selecting the cell or range and pointing to the black border around the cell or range so that the mouse pointer changes from a cross to an arrow. Then drag the cell or range to a new location.

AutoFill

To continue a pattern you have begun, use the fill handle in the lower right corner of a cell or range. For example, if you begin the pattern 0, 5, 10 and want to continue it down a column, select the cells holding these values and click the little black square in the lower right corner of the range. The mouse pointer changes from a white outlined cross to a black cross. Now drag the mouse down the column as far as you want the pattern to go. This procedure also works for easily identifiable patterns of labels, such as months of the year and days of the week.

Charting Your Work

Excel's Chart Wizard allows you to quickly and easily create professional, presentation-quality charts based on worksheet data. This section walks you through the steps you take to work with the Chart Wizard, paying particular attention to how you can use charts as powerful tools for better communicating complex information.

NOTE   *You can use Excel charts in other Office programs, too. Just copy and paste them.*

Understanding Excel's Charting Terms

In order to easily work with Excel's Chart Wizard, you need to learn how Excel views to-be-plotted data and the terminology that Excel uses to refer to the parts of a chart.

How Excel Sees Chart Data

To easily use Excel for charting, you need to learn three key terms: *data points*, *data series*, and *data categories*.

The individual values you plot in a chart are called *data points*. Because a chart visually represents one or more numeric values, data points are always values.

The term *data series* refers to a collection of values that are all related—that are all part of the same set. If you want to plot advertising expenditures over the last 12 months, that collection of expense values is a data series.

Most charts you create use more than one data series. For example, if you want to compare sales revenues of three competitors, each competitor's sales revenues would constitute its own data series. In the worksheet shown in Figure 5-25, you can see the annual sales revenues for three fictitious companies: Anderson Company, Baker Incorporated, and Carson Corporation. The data points that show Anderson's revenue represent a data series. The data points that show Baker's revenue represent another data series. And the data points that represent Carson's revenue represent still a third and final data series.

	A	B	C	D
1		Anderson Company	Baker Incorporated	Carson Corporation
2	January	37,582	25,987	36,550
3	February	28,975	26,320	37,652
4	March	40,250	35,675	39,459
5	April	45,683	42,897	42,009
6	May	35,411	45,997	45,873
7	June	47,005	47,698	50,951

Figure 5-25 A simple worksheet with sales revenue data.

The term *data categories* refers to the secondary perspective on to-be-charted data. If you look at Figure 5-25 again, you can also see January data points, February data points, March data points, and so on. Each month's collection of data points represents a data category. The collection of January data points represents the January data category. Similarly, the February data points represent the February data category. The same thing is true of the March, April, May, and June data points.

In addition to providing data points, data series, and data categories, you need to provide labels that name the data series and the data categories. In Figure 5-25, for example, you can see that cells B1, C1, and D1 hold labels that describe the names of the companies. In cells A2, A3, A4, A5, A6, and A7, you see labels that identify the time intervals used as the data categories. Including data category and data series names in your worksheet is important. If you include this information in your worksheet, it is easily added later to your chart.

Components of Excel Charts

Excel's Chart Wizard and documentation use several charting terms: *data markers, data-marker descriptions, legend, chart text, plot area,* and *chart area.* You will find it useful to understand just what these words and phrases mean, so the following list provides definitions:

- Data markers are the graphical elements used to represent individual data point values in a chart. Figure 5-26, for example, uses symbols, or points, on a line to show data point values.

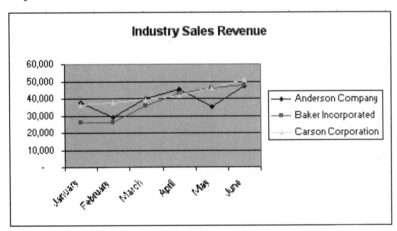

Figure 5-26 A line chart of the sales revenue data shown in Figure 5-25.

- Other types of charts in Excel use other data markers. A chart that uses columns or bars, for example, has column or bar data markers. A pie chart has pie-slice data markers as shown in Figure 5-27, and so on.

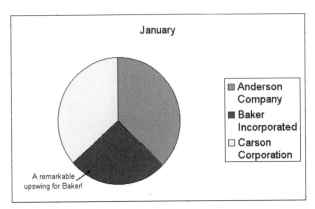

Figure 5-27 A simple pie chart.

- Excel typically describes and qualifies data markers using the data-marker descriptions such as axis scales and data labels. Different types of charts use different data-marker descriptions. Bar, column, and line charts use axis scales. (This is what Figure 5-26 shows, of course.) Pie and doughnut charts use data labels (see Figure 5-27).

- A legend names and identifies the data series you have plotted. In Figure 5-27, the legend names the data series and then shows which colors are used for which pie slices.

- Chart text describes a chart or some part of a chart. Figure 5-26, for example, shows a chart title (Industry Sales Revenue). Figure 5-27 shows an example of a text box such as you might use to provide freeform annotation of a chart.

- The plot area of a chart is the area that includes the data markers and data-marker descriptions. In Figure 5-26, the rectangle that shows the lines and scales represents the plot area. In the chart shown in Figure 5-27, the circle that shows the slices of pie and the data labels that identify the slices of pie comprise the plot area.

- The chart area includes plot area, any chart text, and a legend.

Presenting Data with Charts

Once you understand the terms that Excel uses to describe to-be-charted data and the parts of a chart, you can easily create charts. In essence, you need to simply select the worksheet data you want to chart, indicate where Excel should place the chart, and then tell the Chart Wizard to create the chart.

Using the Chart Wizard

To use the Chart Wizard, first enter your to-be-charted data in an Excel worksheet. As mentioned earlier, you want to include not only the data series' data points but also the appropriate labels. Figure 5-28 shows an example of how you might do this.

	A	B	C	D	E
1		Anderson Company	Baker Incorporated	Carson Corporation	
2	January	37,582	25,987	36,550	
3	February	28,975	26,320	37,652	
4	March	40,250	35,675	39,459	
5	April	45,683	42,897	42,009	
6	May	35,411	45,997	45,873	
7	June	47,005	47,698	50,95	
8					
9					

Figure 5-28   A simple worksheet with data you might plot in a chart.

To create a chart that visually depicts the data in a worksheet, follow these steps:

1. Select the data you want to plot in the chart.

To select the data, select the worksheet range that includes the data series and any data series' names and data categories' names. In Figure 5-28, you would select the worksheet range A1:D7.

NOTE   *If you arrange your data series in the way shown in Figure 5-28, Excel can usually correctly guess what the data series are, what labels show data series' names, and what labels show the data categories' names.*

2. Start the Chart Wizard.

You can do this by clicking the Chart Wizard button on the toolbar or choosing the Insert menu's Chart command. Excel displays the first Chart Wizard dialog box, as shown in Figure 5-29.

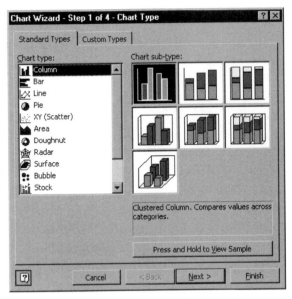

Figure 5-29 The first Chart Wizard dialog box.

3. Select the type of chart you want.

Select one of Excel's chart types from the Chart Type list box. Excel provides 14 different types of charts: Column, Bar, Line, Pie, XY (Scatter), Area, Doughnut, Radar, Surface, Bubble, Stock, Cylinder, Cone, and Pyramid.

TIP *The following section, "Choosing the Right Chart Type," summarizes some of the rules of thumb that people often use to choose a particular chart type.*

4. Select the Chart sub-type.

After you select the Chart type, Excel displays the different versions available for the chart type as clickable buttons in the Chart Sub-type box. Excel displays a short description of the selected chart sub-type in the area below the Chart Sub-type box. To select a chart, click the button that looks like the chart you want. After making your selection, click Next.

NOTE *You can tell Excel to display a rough-draft version of the chart you are creating by clicking the Press And Hold To View Sample button.*

5. Verify that Excel has correctly interpreted the to-be-charted data.

When Excel displays the second Chart Wizard dialog box, as shown in Figure 5-30, use it to verify that Excel is retrieving the correct data from the worksheet (this should be the case if you select the data correctly in step 1) and that it has correctly identified the data series. If Excel hasn't correctly interpreted the to-be-plotted data, click the Worksheet button at the right end of the Data Range text box. When Excel minimizes the Chart Wizard dialog box, reselect the correct range. To restore the Chart Wizard dialog box, click the Worksheet button on the minimized Chart Wizard again. If Excel has misinterpreted how you have organized your worksheet data—Excel assumes the chart has fewer data series than data categories—click the other Series In option button. Click Next when you are finished.

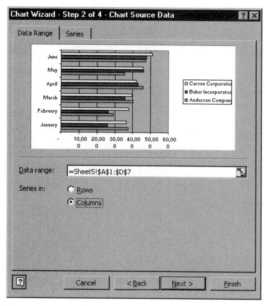

Figure 5-30 The second Chart Wizard dialog box.

NOTE   *You can return to a previous Chart Wizard dialog box by clicking the Back button.*

6. Add chart text as needed.

When Excel displays the third Chart Wizard dialog box, as shown in Figure 5-31, you use its Titles tab to add a chart title and axis titles. To add such chart text, just click the appropriate text box and type the text you want. Click Next when you are finished.

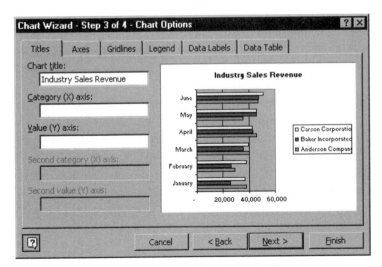

Figure 5-31 The third Chart Wizard dialog box.

NOTE   *Excel updates the chart picture shown on the third Chart Wizard dialog box for any text you add.*

7. Choose a location for the new chart.

Excel lets you place charts either as graphics in a worksheet or in their own individual worksheets. You use the fourth Chart Wizard dialog box, as shown in Figure 5-32, to choose which location you want for your chart.

To place the chart on its own worksheet, click the As New Sheet option button and then enter a name for the new chart sheet. To add the chart as a graphic on an existing worksheet, click the As Object In option button and then select the worksheet from the As Object In drop-down list box. When you complete this step, you have finished creating the chart. Click Finish.

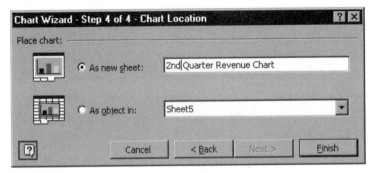

Figure 5-32 The fourth Chart Wizard dialog box.

Figure 5-33 shows how the worksheet data from Figure 5-28 looks in a bar chart that resides on its own chart sheet. To view the chart, click its sheet tab. To print the chart in the selected sheet, simply click the Print toolbar button or choose the File menu's Print command.

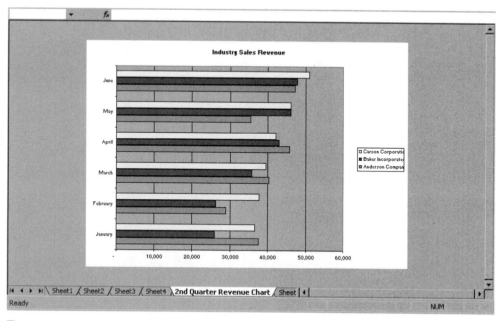

Figure 5-33 A bar chart on a chart sheet.

Figure 5-34 shows the same worksheet data as that shown in Figure 5-33, except this time the worksheet data is depicted in a column chart that is placed as an object in a worksheet. You can resize any worksheet object, including a chart, by clicking the object and then dragging the square selection handles that appear on the sides and corners of the object.

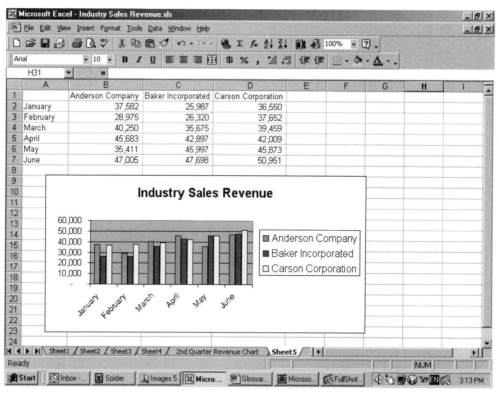

Figure 5-34 A column chart object in a worksheet.

To print a free-floating chart object, click it and then click the Print toolbar button or choose the File menu's Print command. You can also print the chart object by printing the worksheet over which it floats.

Choosing the Right Chart Type

Choosing the appropriate chart type is probably at least as much art as science. Nevertheless, it is still worthwhile to briefly discuss the basic data comparison that you want a chart to make, and the principal message that you want a chart to communicate. All three factors greatly affect your choice of a chart type.

Data Comparisons That Charts Make

Charts allow you to visually compare data in five basic ways, which means that your first step in determining the appropriate chart type is often simply to consider what data comparison you want to make. Suppose, for example, that you have collected detailed product sales revenue data for a golf equipment manufacturer. Using a chart, you might decide to look at this data in any of the ways summarized in Table 5-3.

COMPARISON	DESCRIPTION	CHART TYPES
Part-to-whole	Compares an individual data point value to the sum of a data series. Comparing sales of a particular golf club set to total sales, for example, is a part-to-whole comparison.	Pie Chart Doughnut Chart Area Chart
Whole-to-whole	Compares individual data point values to each other or data series to each other. Comparing sales of a starter men's golf club set to a starter women's golf club set, for example, is a whole-to-whole comparison.	Bar Chart Cylinder Chart Cone Chart Pyramid Chart Doughnut Chart Radar Chart
Time-series	Compares data point values from different time periods to show how values change over time. Showing monthly sales over the last year, for example, is a time-series comparison.	Column Chart Line Chart Cylinder Chart Cone Chart Pyramid Chart
Correlation	Compares different data series to explore correlation between the data series. Comparing industry-wide sales to the average age of the population, for example, is a correlation comparison.	Scatter Chart Bubble Chart Surface Chart

Table 5-3   Summary of the four data comparisons made in charts.

Importance of the Chart's Essential Message

An important factor to consider is exactly what message you want to visually communicate with your chart. Typically, you can use the message as the chart title. But beyond this, you may want to experiment with different chart types and sub-types to see which best support your message.

NOTE   *Of course, a chart can and should also be used to visually explore data. Oftentimes, information that is hidden in raw, tabular presentations of data suddenly becomes visible once you depict the data in a chart. This point is worth mentioning because when you are exploring data—something you might do by viewing data in different chart types—there probably shouldn't be any rules. Quite literally, thinking "outside the box" might often mean that you want to examine your data in unusual ways.*

Customizing Your Charts

You can easily customize your charts so they better fit your needs. You can, for example, rerun the Chart Wizard. This approach is usually simplest. But you can also use Chart menu commands to change specific elements of a chart. The paragraphs that follow discuss each of the two approaches, because you will find occasion to use both.

Using the Chart Wizard to Customize a Chart

To use the Chart Wizard to customize a chart, select the chart and then click the Chart Wizard toolbar button. Excel restarts the Chart Wizard, and you can step through the four dialog boxes (described earlier in the section "Using the Chart Wizard") to make your changes.

Using the Shortcut Menu's Format Command

There is another way to change some element of a chart. Right-click the part of the chart that you want to change and then choose Format from the shortcut menu. For example, if you want to change the scaling of the values axis, you can right-click the values axis and then choose the Format Axis command. (Obviously, if you right-click other parts of a chart, Excel displays a different Format command which, in turn, displays a different dialog box.) You can make only a handful of changes to each part of a chart:

- Patterns—Many of the Format dialog boxes display a Patterns tab that you can use to select the colors and lines you want Excel to use to draw the chart object.

- Fonts—Any Format dialog box for an element that includes text provides a Font tab that you can use to choose font, font style, font point size, and special text effects.

- Number—Any Format dialog box for an element that includes numbers provides a Number tab that you can use to choose a numeric formatting style.

- Alignment—Any Format dialog box for an element that includes text provides an Alignment tab that you can use to align text.

- Scale—The Format dialog box for both the axes and the gridlines provides a Scale tab that you can use to specify how Excel should calibrate and draw the axis or grid.

TIP   *Remember that if you have a question about how to work with some dialog box option, you can click the Help button and then click the option to get a brief but usually very helpful description. The Help button appears in the upper right corner of the dialog box and is marked with a question mark.*

Skill 6

USE POWERPOINT FOR POWERFUL PRESENTATIONS

Featuring:

- PowerPoint Terminology
- Creating Your Presentation
- Enhancing Your Presentation
- Polishing Your Slide Show
- Guidelines to Effective Presentations

Consider this scenario: The CEO calls you in and compliments you on the work you did on a recent hurry-up project. And, because you did such a great job, he wants you to present it to the stockholders meeting next month. No holds barred; it needs to be a knock-your-socks-off presentation. Where to go? What to do? You know the subject inside and out, but how do you make the stockholders stand up and say "Wow!"?

Never fear, Microsoft Office's PowerPoint is the application you need and with the techniques you learn in this skill, you can create the presentation that makes the impression you want.

PowerPoint Terminology

PowerPoint is an easy application to learn, but first you need to understand some basic PowerPoint terms:

- Slide—The slide is the essential element of a presentation, as shown in Figure 6-1. Although most PowerPoint presentations today are presented electronically with a computer connected to other computers or a projector, most presentations used to use 35mm slides and slide projectors. The terminology has carried through. You can still have 35mm slides prepared, if you choose, or overhead transparencies; but whatever your delivery medium, each screen you create is called a slide.

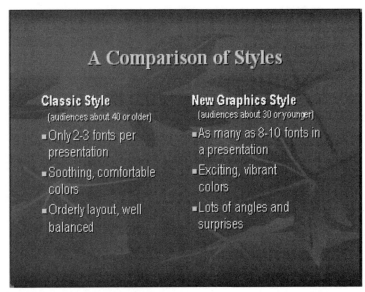

Figure 6-1   A PowerPoint slide.

- Title Slide—The Title Slide is usually the first slide that you have in your presentation. It frequently has a slightly different arrangement of text and graphics from the regular slides so that it stands out, much like the title page of a book or report.

- Master Slide—The Master Slide is the plan for how your slides look. Any text or graphic that is placed on the Master Slide, by default, is shown on all slides in a presentation. On the Master Slide, you set Text Font, Size, and Color. You set the arrangement of text objects for all slides. In addition to the Slide Master, which is the plan for all regular slides, you may have a Title Master, which sets the parameters for your Title Slide (or slides).

- Presentation—This is the completed product, the collection of all the slides put together in an organized, informative manner. The presentation can be printed on paper as a hard copy presentation, it can be printed on transparency stock to use with an overhead projector, it can be printed as 35mm slides for use in a slide projector, or it can be run from a computer to other computer screens or to a LCD projector.

- Object—An object is any single component of a slide. You can have a text object, a clip art object, an AutoShape object, and so on.

- Animation—Animation in PowerPoint is an attention-getting way to enhance your presentation. Remarkable animations are included within PowerPoint, such as text or clip art flying onto the screen or following a motion path around the screen. Of course, animation works only with onscreen presentations, but with it you can add pizzazz to any computer slide show.

- Transition—Transition is a type of animation, but transitions specifically govern the way one slide changes into the next. Transitions may be very simple (sliding in from the right or left) or may be very dramatic (eight-spoke wheel spinning to reveal new slide).

Defining PowerPoint Views

A view is one of the several ways of looking at your presentation within the PowerPoint program. To change a view, choose a different view from the View menu. The following three views are used the most:

- Normal view—This view places one slide at a time in the PowerPoint window with toolbars and the Outline/Preview pane to the left side of the screen, as shown in Figure 6-2. In this view you can edit text and apply graphics.

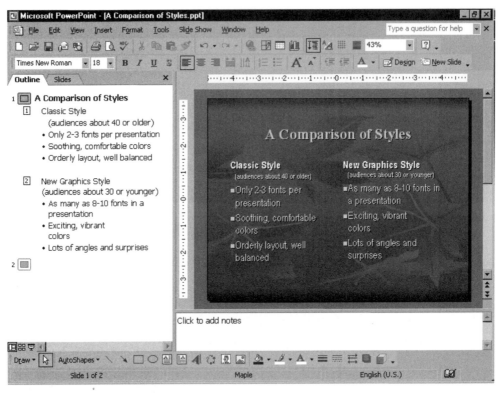

Figure 6-2   The PowerPoint window in Normal view.

- Slide Sorter view—The Slide Sorter view places all the slides, in miniature, in the PowerPoint window, as shown in Figure 6-3. You cannot edit individual slides in this view, but you can easily reorder them by dragging them from one place to another with the mouse.

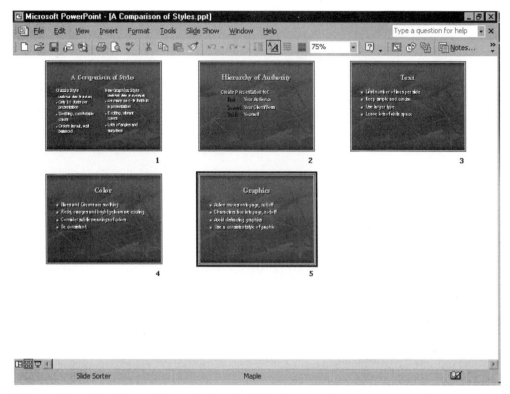

Figure 6-3   The PowerPoint window in Slide Sorter view.

- Slide Show view—The Slide Show view shows the presentation, one slide at a time, on the computer screen all by itself. This is the view that you use to show the final product to your audience if you are preparing a computer display presentation. It can be manually controlled by using the mouse or the keyboard, or it can be set to run automatically with predetermined timings.

Creating Your Presentation

PowerPoint provides several ways of approaching the creation of your presentation. For example, you could use the AutoContent Wizard that is part of the PowerPoint program. The AutoContent Wizard asks you some questions, lets you make some choices, and produces a presentation for you. All you need to do is enter text and fine-tune it to your specifications. Another way would be to outline what you want to say on the Outline pane and let it determine the slides that you want to use. You can also create an outline in Microsoft Word and open it in PowerPoint to have a presentation created from your outline. A third way is to build your presentation one slide at a time, manually entering text and layout. In this section, we take a look at all three of these ways to create a presentation.

Using the AutoContent Wizard

By far the easiest way to jump-start your presentation, AutoContent Wizard does most of the work for you. Not all presentations are suited to the use of the wizard, but for those that are, it is a powerful tool. Follow these steps:

1. Select From AutoContent Wizard from the New Presentation pane.

If you have just started PowerPoint, the New Presentation pane is displayed to the right of your screen. If you do not see the New Presentation pane, choose the File menu's New command and the pane appears. Then select From AutoContent Wizard in the New section. The AutoContent Wizard Start window is displayed, as shown in Figure 6-4.

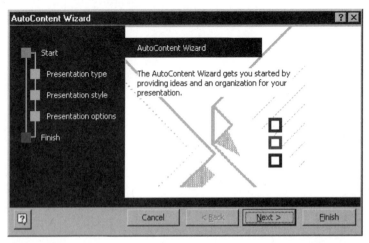

Figure 6-4   The Start window of the AutoContent Wizard.

2. Click Next.

The Start window provides information on AutoContent Wizard. Click Next and the Presentation Type window is displayed, as shown in Figure 6-5.

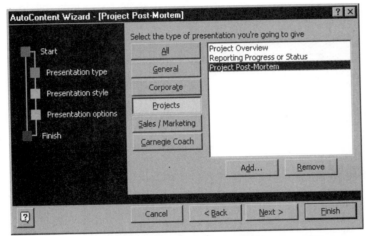

Figure 6-5 The Presentation Type window of the AutoContent Wizard.

3. Select the type of presentation you are going to give.

The Presentation Type window provides numerous presentation types divided into categories. Choose a category from the buttons and then click the presentation type in the field to the right. (For our scenario, we select the Projects category and the Projects Post-mortem type.) After you have made your selection, click Next to move to the Presentation Style window, as shown in Figure 6-6.

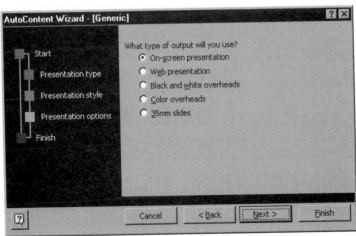

Figure 6-6 The Presentation Style window of the AutoContent Wizard.

4. Select the type of output you will use.

To properly configure your presentation to the final output medium, select one of the Styles listed in the Presentation Style window. Figure 6-6 shows the selection of an On-screen Presentation. Then click Next to move to the next step in the Wizard, the Presentation Options window, as shown in Figure 6-7.

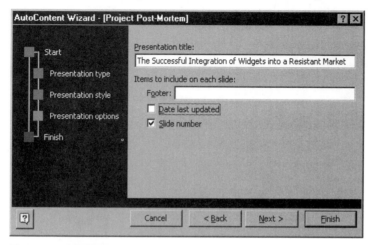

Figure 6-7   The Presentation Options window of the AutoContent Wizard.

5. Enter the necessary data.

Type in the presentation title in the field provided. Also, consider what information you want to show on every slide, such as Date Last Updated, Slide Number, or other footer information. Make the appropriate selections, and click Next to display the Finish window, as shown in Figure 6-8.

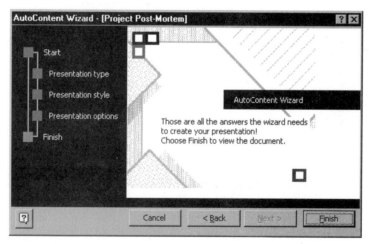

Figure 6-8   The Finish window of the AutoContent Wizard.

6. Click Finish.

Clicking Finish displays your completed presentation, as shown in Figure 6-9. Notice that the author's name is displayed on the Title Slide. The computer pulls this information from user data established at the installation of Office. If the name that is displayed is not accurate, you can change it by highlighting the text in either the Outline pane or on the slide itself and entering the correct information.

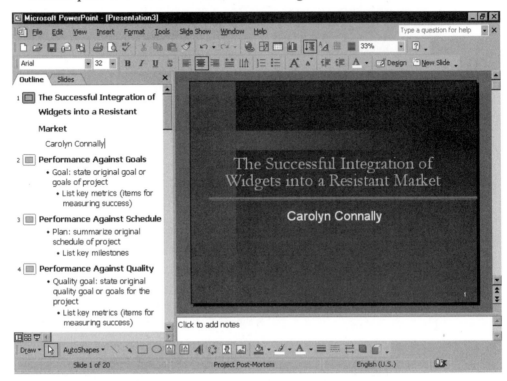

Figure 6-9   The presentation completed by AutoContent Wizard.

7. Edit the presentation.

The text of the presentation is composed of suggestions of appropriate data to include in the presentation. Quite obviously, you need to use your own text in its place. Additionally, the presentation may be enhanced using techniques discussed later in this chapter.

Using the Outline Pane

Although the AutoContent Wizard is the fastest way to create a presentation, many people prefer to work from an outline. PowerPoint provides a powerful outline tool that you can use to create your presentation. Follow these steps:

1. Open the Outline pane.

By default, the Outline pane appears in your PowerPoint window to the left of the slide display, as shown in Figure 6-10. If the Outline pane is not displayed, choose the View menu's Normal command and the Outline pane appears. There are two tabs on this pane: one showing the outline of your presentation, the other showing previews of the slides that currently make up the presentation. Click the Outline tab.

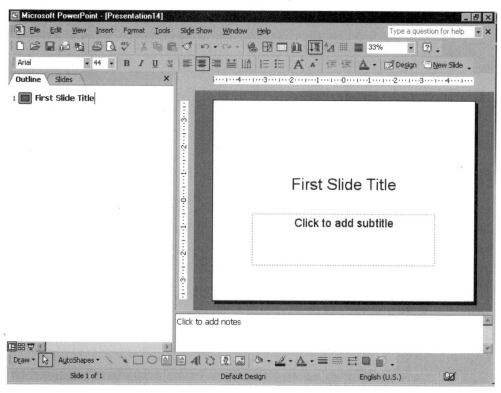

Figure 6-10 The PowerPoint window displaying the Outline pane.

2. Compose your outline.

In the Outline pane, create an outline with the exact text you want in your presentation using these guidelines:

- The first level of text is a slide title; subsequent levels of text are bullet points on that slide.

- Subordinate levels can be achieved by pressing the Tab key.

- To reverse that action and make a line of text a higher level, press Shift+Tab.

- You can create as many levels as you need, but keep in mind that more than three may confuse your audience.

- Keep each slide's text to a minimum.

- Notice that your outline text is being placed on a slide in the Slide Display window.

3. **Edit or enhance your presentation.**

Fine-tuning your presentation can take place on the Outline pane or on the slides themselves. In the Outline pane, edit text using standard word-processing techniques (see "Skill 4: Use Word for Document Generation"). To change text on the slides, just click the text first to select the text box, as shown in Figure 6-11, and then use word-processing techniques.

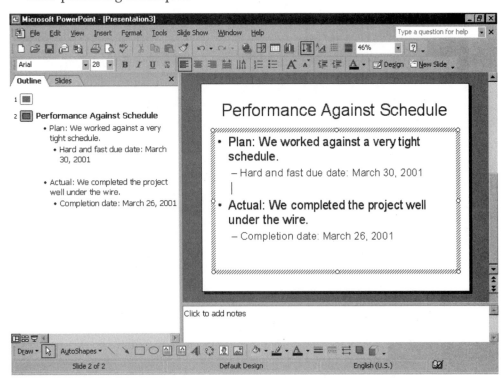

Figure 6-11 Clicking selects the text box.

To further augment your work, see "Enhancing Your Presentation," below.

Importing an Outline from Word

If you have an outline already developed in Word, there is no need to re-create it. In PowerPoint, just use the File menu's Open command, locate the folder, and double-click the outline file. A new presentation is created in PowerPoint based on the Word document. Here, too, the first level of the outline becomes a slide; subsequent levels are the text on that slide. Use the same techniques discussed above to adjust the text levels.

Enhancing Your Presentation

The effectiveness of a presentation is increased by the layout of the slides. Although you should keep the adornments appropriate to your audience and subject matter, clip art, graphics, and layout design are usually a good way to add punch to your presentation and keep audience attention. The following sections describe some of the techniques you can use to do so.

Applying a Design Template

Although you may create a background design yourself (see "Customizing the Master Slide," below), PowerPoint comes packed with numerous design templates that you can apply to your presentation. You want to do this for sure if you created your presentation from outline, because there will be no design applied automatically. When you use the AutoContent Wizard to create your slide presentation, however, a design template is automatically applied, but it can be changed. To apply a design template to your presentation, follow these steps:

1. **Display the Slide Design pane.**

   Choose the Format menu's Slide Design command. The Slide Design pane opens to the right of your slide view, as shown in Figure 6-12.

Figure 6-12 The Slide Design pane.

2. Select Design Templates.

The design templates may already be displayed at the bottom of the pane (see Figure 6-12). If not, click the Design Templates link.

3. Select a design template.

You can have fun with this. When you click a design template from the previews in the Slide Design pane, the design is automatically applied to your slide, as shown in Figure 6-13. If you are considering a change to a presentation with a template already applied, don't hesitate to try a new look. If you don't like the results, you can find the original design under the Recently Used category at the top of the display.

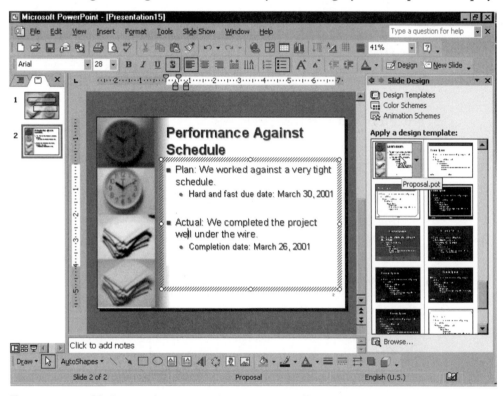

Figure 6-13 Clicking a design template automatically applies it to your presentation.

4. Save your presentation.

After you have applied a design template to your presentation, it is important to save that change. Just click the Save button on the toolbar. If you have already named and saved the presentation, the save occurs in the background. If your presentation has not yet been saved, of course, you are asked to name it and save it to the desired folder.

Adding Clip Art and AutoShape Graphics

Even for the most reserved and conservative of audiences, adding graphics to your presentation helps break up the monotony of text alone. You can use the clip art that comes with PowerPoint, you can use clip art from anywhere on your hard drive, or you can create the graphic by using PowerPoint's AutoShapes.

Inserting Clip Art from Media Gallery

To insert a clip from the software that comes with PowerPoint, follow these steps:

1. Display the slide.

Start by displaying the slide where you want the clip art to appear.

2. Open the Insert ClipArt pane.

Choose the Insert Menu's Picture command, and then choose Clip Art. The Insert Clip Art pane appears to the right of your slide.

3. Enter text, and start the search.

In the Search Text box, enter a descriptive word or phrase for the graphic you want to find. Click the Search button.

TIP   *The Media Gallery is capable of holding an unlimited amount of graphics, photos, sound files, and videos, so you can add files you have acquired through outside sources. Although you can add clips and other media to your presentation from anyplace on your hard drive, the Media Gallery offers you an excellent location for sorting and locating the files you want.*

4. Select the clip.

From the clip art displayed in the Insert Clip Art pane, select the graphic that is most suited to your presentation. The clip art is placed on your slide, as shown in Figure 6-14.

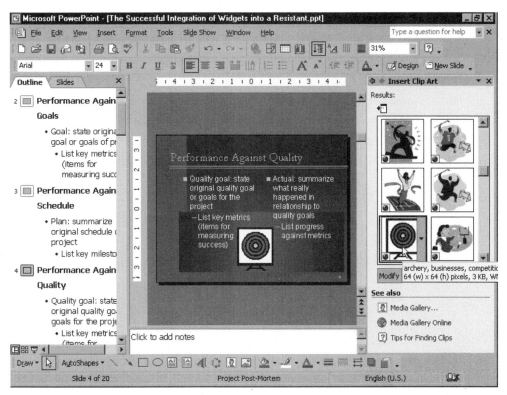

Figure 6-14 Selecting a graphic from the Insert Clip Art pane places that graphic on your slide.

5. Arrange the graphic.

After the graphic is located on your slide, you can size it or arrange it for the best result by using the following methods:

- Move a graphic—When you place your mouse pointer over the graphic, it changes into a four-pointed arrow. Just click and drag the graphic to place it in the best location.

- Size a graphic—When you click once on the graphic to select it, sizing handles (little round dots) appear along the sides, top, and bottom of the clip. With your mouse, grab one of the handles and drag to enlarge or reduce the graphic. Dragging one of the corner handles enlarges or reduces the picture proportionately. Using one of the side handles stretches the picture and distorts it from its original proportions.

- Arrange the graphic's order—When clip art is first inserted into a slide, it is, by default, placed as the top layer of all the other items on the slide. If you want the graphic to be tucked in behind another layout element, you can change its level. From the Drawing toolbar, as shown in Figure 6-15, choose Draw, choose Order, and then choose Send To Back (which puts it at the very bottom of all of the layout elements) or Send Backward (which places the picture one layer further down each time you select it). If you want to bring a picture forward among the layers, use the Bring To Front or Bring Forward commands.

Figure 6-15 The Drawing toolbar displaying the Order menu.

NOTE   *The Drawing toolbar, by default, is located at the bottom of the screen. However, if your Drawing toolbar is not visible, right-click any toolbar and choose Drawing from the shortcut menu.*

Inserting Clip Art from File

Clip art that you have stored on your hard drive in folders other than Media Gallery is just as easily incorporated into your slides. To insert a clip from a file, follow these steps:

1. **Display the slide.**

   Start by displaying the slide where you want the clip to appear.

2. **Open the Insert Picture dialog box.**

   Choose the Insert Menu's Picture command, and then choose From File. The Insert Picture dialog box opens, as shown in Figure 6-16.

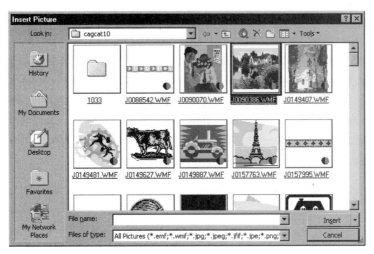

Figure 6-16 The Insert Picture dialog box.

3. Select the graphic file.

Using the list, locate the file that you want to insert into your slide. Double-click or click to select it and then click the Insert button. The graphic is inserted into the slide.

4. Arrange the graphic.

After the graphic is located in your slide, you can size it or arrange it for the best result by using the following methods:

- Move a graphic—When you place your mouse pointer over the graphic, it changes into a four-pointed arrow. Just click and drag the graphic to place it in the best location.

- Size a graphic—When you click once on the graphic to select it, sizing handles (little round dots) appear along the sides, top, and bottom of the clip. With your mouse, grab one of the handles and drag to enlarge or reduce the graphic. Dragging one of the corner handles enlarges or reduces the picture proportionately. Using one of the side handles stretches the picture and distorts it from its original proportions.

- Arrange the graphic's order—When clip art is first inserted into a slide, it is, by default, placed as the top layer of all the other items on the slide. If you want the graphic to be tucked in behind another layout element, you can change its level. From the Drawing toolbar, select Draw and then select Order, as shown in Figure 6-15. Choose Send To Back (which puts it at the very bottom of all of the layout elements) or Send Backward (which places the picture one layer further down each time you select it). If you want to bring a picture forward among the layers, use the Bring To Front or Bring Forward commands.

Adding AutoShape Graphics

If you are speaking to a conservative or sophisticated audience, such as a Board of Directors, you want to keep your graphics as simple as possible. Sometimes PowerPoint's AutoShape graphics are just what you need.

AutoShape graphics are simple forms that you choose from a menu and drag to create, making them the size and proportion that is right for you. To use this convenient PowerPoint feature, follow these steps:

1. Open the AutoShape menu.

Click the AutoShape button on the Drawing toolbar. The AutoShape menu is displayed, as shown in Figure 6-17.

Figure 6-17 The AutoShape menu.

TIP   *The AutoShape menu can float freely on your screen. This is particularly useful if you are going to be using it a lot. Floating it saves your having to click the Drawing toolbar when you want to choose from the AutoShapes.*

2. Select an AutoShape category.

From the seven AutoShape categories, click the category that would contain the shape you are looking for.

3. Select an AutoShape.

From the pop-up menu, select the AutoShape of your choice. The pop-up menu and the AutoShape menu close, leaving your mouse pointer in the shape of a cross, as shown in Figure 6-18.

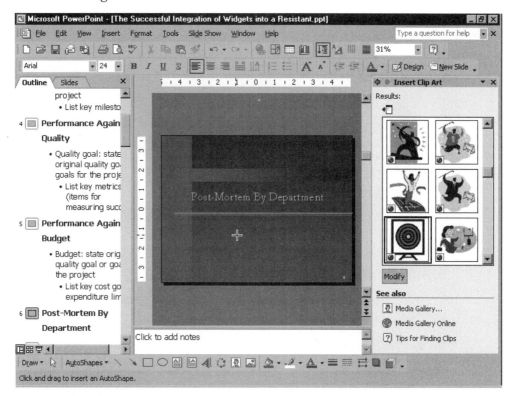

Figure 6-18 The mouse pointer prepared to insert an AutoShape graphic.

4. Insert the AutoShape.

Place your mouse pointer on your slide where you want the shape to be located. Click and drag to insert the shape, adjusted to the proportions you want, as shown in Figure 6-19.

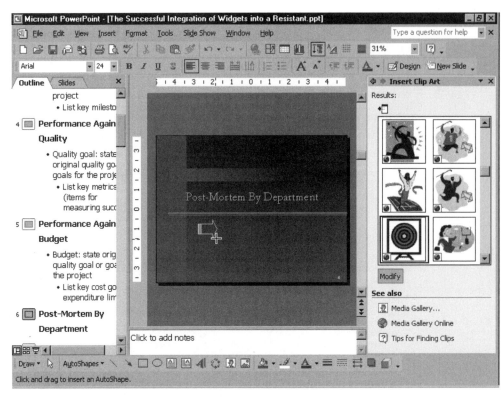

Figure 6-19 Drawing the AutoShape on a slide.

5. Adjust the AutoShape.

AutoShapes can be sized or moved like any other graphic. Click and drag to move. Click and drag a sizing handle to enlarge or reduce.

6. Add color to your AutoShape.

If you have a slide design applied to your slide, the AutoShape will automatically be filled with a color complementary to your color scheme. To change the color or fill in a noncolored AutoShape, select the graphic, click the Fill Color button on the Drawing toolbar, and select a color. The graphic is filled with the selected color, as shown in Figure 6-20.

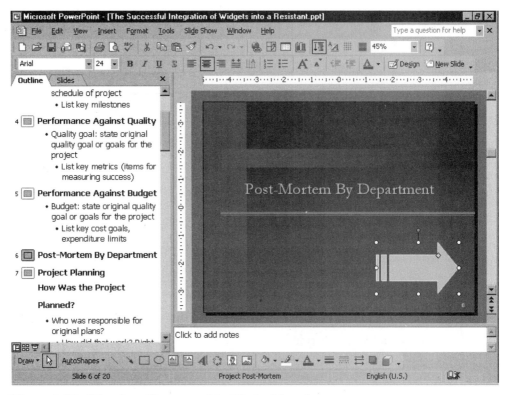

Figure 6-20 The AutoShape graphic filled with color.

Using Mini Applications to Add Objects

PowerPoint comes with several mini applications that allow you to insert certain objects into your slides. Using the mini application is a far simpler job than trying to create the object yourself.

WordArt

WordArt is a remarkable program that allows you to create artistic shapes with text. To insert a WordArt object into your slide, follow these steps:

1. Start the WordArt program.

Click the WordArt button (it looks like a large, tilted, blue A) on the Drawing toolbar to open the WordArt Gallery, as shown in Figure 6-21.

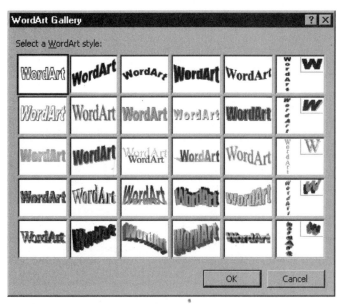

Figure 6-21 The WordArt Gallery.

2. Select a WordArt style.

From the many styles presented in the WordArt Gallery, select the one that most closely meets your needs. It can be adjusted if it is not exactly right. Then click OK. The Edit WordArt Text dialog box is displayed, as shown in Figure 6-22.

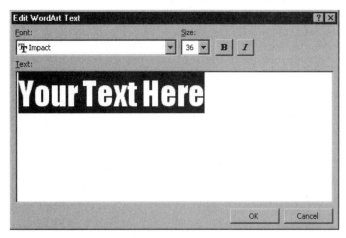

Figure 6-22 The Edit WordArt Text dialog box.

3. Enter WordArt text.

The words *Your Text Here* are already highlighted in the Edit WordArt Text dialog box. All you have to do is type in the text you want, and click OK. The WordArt object is placed on the slide, as shown in Figure 6-23.

Figure 6-23 A WordArt object placed on a slide.

4. Adjust the WordArt object.

Just like other graphics, you need to adjust a WordArt object to the size and position that works best in the presentation. Click the object to display the sizing handles; drag one of the handles to resize your WordArt. Click and drag the object with your mouse to reposition it.

In addition to the sizing handles, a WordArt object can have other handles (colored bright yellow) that otherwise adjust the shape of the WordArt. For example, a WordArt object in which the letters are slanted may have a yellow handle that adjusts the degree of the slant. Just click and drag the yellow handle to see the effect.

Diagram

The Diagram mini application allows you to choose one of six diagram formats:

- Organization Chart—Used to show hierarchical relationships.

- Cycle Diagram—Used to demonstrate process with a continuous cycle.

- Radial Diagram—Shows the relationships of a core element.

- Pyramid Diagram—Portrays foundation-based relationships.

- Venn Diagram—Shows areas of overlap between elements.

- Target Diagram—Shows steps toward a goal.

To place one of these helpful diagrams in your presentation, follow these steps:

1. **Display the slide.**

   Make sure that the slide on which you want to insert the diagram is active.

2. **Open the Diagram Gallery.**

   Choose the Insert menu's Diagram command. The Diagram Gallery opens displaying graphics representing the six diagrams from which you may choose, as shown in Figure 6-24.

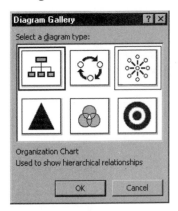

Figure 6-24 The Diagram Gallery.

3. **Select the diagram.**

   Clicking a diagram identifies the function of that diagram in the lower portion of the Diagram Gallery window. Select the diagram that best meets your needs, and click OK. The diagram is inserted into your slide.

4. **Adjust the diagram.**

   Like any graphic, a diagram can be moved and sized. It can also be altered to reflect the data you are presenting. Here's how:

   - Move the diagram—Place your mouse pointer over the graphic. The mouse pointer turns into a four-headed arrow. Then click and drag the diagram to a new location.

   - Size the diagram—When you click the diagram once with your mouse, sizing handles appear. However, these sizing handles are configured differently from other graphics. Instead of little dots, they are lines reflecting the sides (straight lines) and the corners (bent lines). Any one of these lines can be grasped with the mouse and dragged to increase or decrease the size. Using the side handles stretches the size of the box in which the diagram is displayed, but does not distort the graphic itself.

- Add labels—Each of the diagrams has provision for labeling its elements, but each does this in its own way. For example, to label the Target Diagram, click any of the callout lines and a box appears for you to enter the label data. In the Venn Diagram, each of the overlapping circles has a box for labeling, but it cannot be seen until you click it. Just click around, and when you see the box, then type, as shown in Figure 6-25.

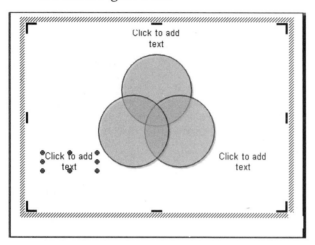

Figure 6-25 A Venn diagram with a label box selected.

- Add shapes—The diagrams are fully adjustable to represent any number of data series. Just right-click in the diagram area, and choose Add Shape from the shortcut menu.

Chart

Chart is a mini application that is very similar to the chart function in Excel. You can use it to insert a chart or graph into your presentation, or you can create one in Excel and copy and paste it into PowerPoint. To use Chart, follow these steps:

1. Display the slide.

Make sure that the slide on which you want to insert the graph is active.

2. Insert a chart into the slide.

Choose the Insert menu's Chart command. A sample chart is placed in your slide and a data sheet is opened on top, as shown in Figure 6-26. The data sheet contains sample data.

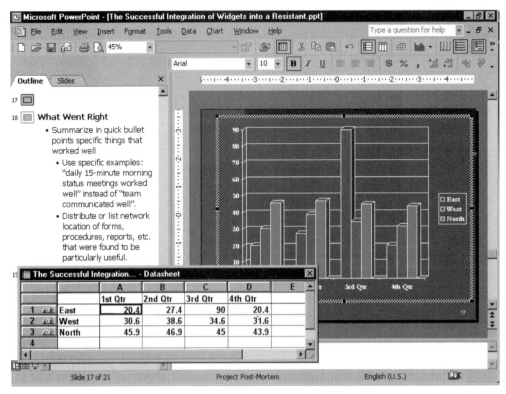

Figure 6-26 A sample chart opened with a sample data sheet on top of it.

3. Edit the data sheet.

Replace the information in the data sheet with labels and values of your own, adding or subtracting columns or rows as necessary. Notice that the chart changes as you edit the data, as shown in Figure 6-27. Also notice that the Standard toolbar changes to a Chart toolbar.

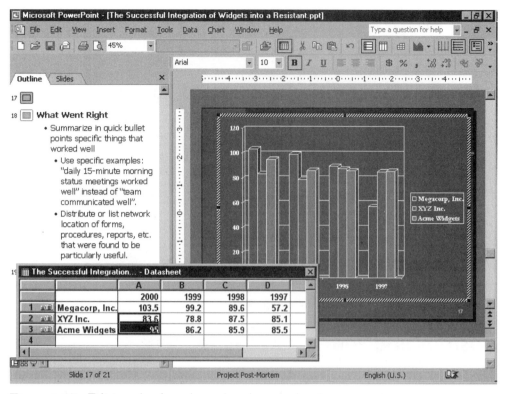

Figure 6-27 Editing the data sheet also changes the chart.

4. Turn off Chart.

Click off of the chart area within the slide. Chart is turned off, and the data sheet closes, as shown in Figure 6-28. To reposition your chart, drag it to a new location on the slide with the mouse.

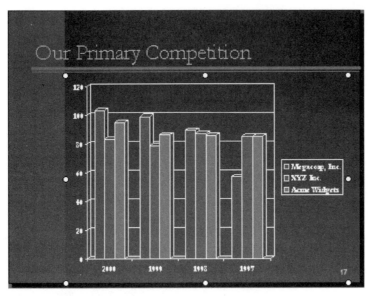

Figure 6-28 The completed chart in the slide.

Customizing Your Master Slide

A Master Slide is the blueprint for all of the slides based on it in the presentation. Objects that show on every slide are held there. A good example would be a company logo that you want to appear on each slide. The Master Slide also dictates the arrangement of text as well as the type face, size, and color.

There are, by default, two Master Slides. One is the Slide Master, the other the Title Master. If you want to change an object on your title slide, you would use the Title Master. All other slides would be affected by the Slide Master. The techniques of editing both Master Slides are the same. To edit the Slide Master or Title Master, follow these steps:

1. Access the Master Slide.

Choose the View menu's Master command, and then choose Slide Master. The Master view is displayed, as shown in Figure 6-29.

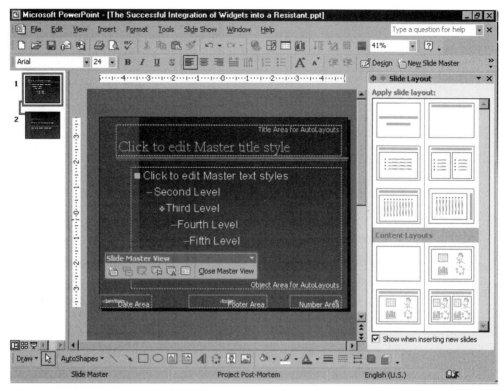

Figure 6-29 The Master View window showing the Slide Master.

2. Choose the Slide Master or Title Master.

From the Preview pane to the left of the window, select the Slide Master or the Title Master. The Slide Master is usually the top one with the Title Master below it. To be certain which is which, click on one preview and its name appears in the status bar at the bottom of the screen. The selected Master also appears in the main window.

3. Edit the Master.

After the Master appears in the PowerPoint window, you can select and edit any of the elements on it. Just keep in mind that anything you place on the Master affects all of the slides that are based on it. Here are some of the areas you may want to adjust:

- Date Area—This area, found in the lower left of the Master Slide, allows you to place a date on your slides. This is probably not as important for an onscreen slide show as it is for a printed presentation. Click where it says <Date/Time>, and enter the appropriate date.

- Footer Area—Found in the center of the lower edge of the Master Slide, the footer allows you to place any text that needs to be on all slides. An example might be the company name or the word *Confidential*. Click the <footer> text, and enter your information.

- Number Area—It is sometimes helpful to have slides numbered. This area adds a number to your slides automatically. In our example, we chose to have the pages numbered during the AutoContent Wizard. If this is not turned on, however, you can do so by choosing the Insert menu's Slide Number command.

- Text Face, Size, and Color—To establish the text scheme for the presentation, click the text block you want to format. Using the Formatting toolbar, select the typeface, size, and color you want to use.

- Bullets for Levels—In the lower text box on the Master, the bullets that are used for five levels of bulleted points are shown. If you want to edit this list (change the bullets), click the level you want to edit and then choose the Format menu's Bullets And Numbering command. Click the Bulleted tab, if necessary, and then select the bullet you want from the list. Click OK.

- Graphics and Background—In addition to the elements mentioned above, you can change the slide design by selecting any design object, including clip art, and editing it as you wish. To add new graphics to the Master, choose the Insert menu's Picture command and then choose either the Clip Art command to take you to the Media Gallery or the From File command to allow you to locate the graphic on your hard drive or from a floppy disk.

4. Close the Master view.

After you have edited the Master Slide to your satisfaction, click the Close Master View button on the Slide Master toolbar. Or, choose the View menu's Normal command. If the slides don't look like you want them to, just repeat the process and edit the Master Slide again.

Polishing Your Slide Show

You've created your presentation. All the data is shown in the most effective way. Now you need to jazz-up the onscreen presentation (also called the Slide Show in PowerPoint) with special effects to make it even more memorable. The following Slide Show effects do just that.

Adding Transitions

A transition is the way one slide leads into another. This can be as simple as one slide disappearing and another taking its place or it can be a very elaborate transition, such as the old slide dissolving into the new one or an eight-spoke wheel turning to reveal the next slide. Transitions are easy to affix to individual slides or to the entire presentation. To affix transitions, follow these steps:

1. Open the Slide Transition pane.

Choose the Slide Show menu's Transition command. The Slide Transition pane opens to the right of your screen, as shown in Figure 6-30.

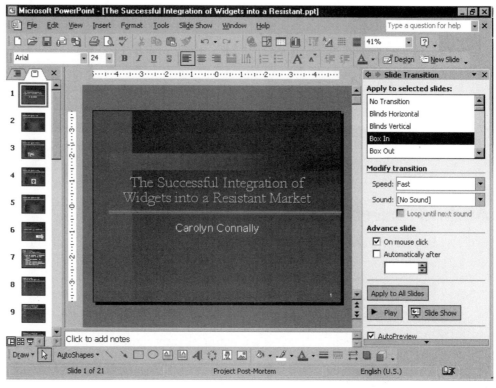

Figure 6-30 The PowerPoint window displaying the Slide Transition pane.

2. Select a slide.

From the Preview pane to the left of your screen, click the slide to which you want to apply a transition. If you want to apply the transition to all slides in the presentation, it doesn't matter which slide is selected.

3. **Select a transition.**

From the Apply To Selected Slides menu on the Slide Transition pane, select a transition. As you click a transition, its effect is demonstrated on the selected slide.

4. **Modify the transition.**

Here is where you establish how quickly you want to transition from one slide to another and what sounds you want to be associated with it. From the Speed menu select Slow, Medium, or Fast. The effect and speed is demonstrated on the slide.

From the Sound menu, select the sound you want from the sounds available on your computer. This is demonstrated, as well. If you want to keep the sound looping until the next sound, select the check box. This is briefly demonstrated but is cut short.

5. **Choose slide advance settings.**

If you want to control when the slide advances, select the On Mouse Click check box. If you want to set a time for the slide to advance, select the Automatically After check box. If both are selected, the slide is advanced by a mouse click or after the determined number of seconds or minutes have elapsed.

6. **Add transitions to the remainder of your presentation.**

If you want to set the same transition for all slides, click the Apply To All Slides button. Otherwise, select another slide and repeat the process.

Adding PowerPoint Animation

PowerPoint animation is not as sophisticated as Mickey Mouse marching and singing across the screen. However, it is a clever way to maintain attention, emphasize points, and dress up your presentation. For best results, use in restraint.

Animation Schemes

Animation Schemes are sets of animation already configured by PowerPoint. available for you to apply to a slide or your entire presentation. These schemes include transitions, so you do not need to set transitions on those slides to which you are applying animation schemes.

1. **Open the Animation Schemes pane.**

Choose the Slide Show menu's Animation Schemes command. The Slide Design pane appears with Animation Schemes selected, as shown in Figure 6-31.

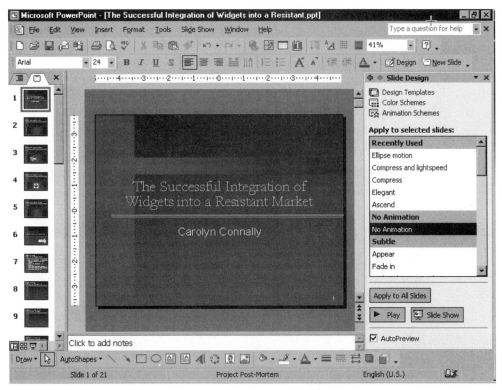

Figure 6-31 The PowerPoint window with the Slide Design pane displayed.

2. Select a slide.

From the Preview pane to the left of your screen, click the slide to which you want to apply an Animation Scheme. If you want to apply the same animation to all slides in the presentation, it doesn't matter which slide is selected.

3. Select an Animation Scheme.

From the Apply To Selected Slides menu on the Slide Design pane, select an Animation Scheme. As you click a scheme, its effect is demonstrated on the selected slide. The schemes are grouped by the following categories: Recently Used, No Animation, Subtle, Moderate, and Exciting. Consider your audience, and select a scheme accordingly

4. Add animation to the remainder of your presentation.

If you want to set the same transition for all slides, click the Apply To All Slides button. Otherwise, select another slide and repeat the process.

Custom Animation

Custom Animation allows you to set specific actions to specific objects on a slide. These settings are set slide by slide. Because individual objects must be selected on each slide, there is no Apply To All Slides command.

1. Open the Animation Schemes pane.

Choose the Slide Show menu's Custom Animation command. The Custom Animation pane appears, as shown in Figure 6-32.

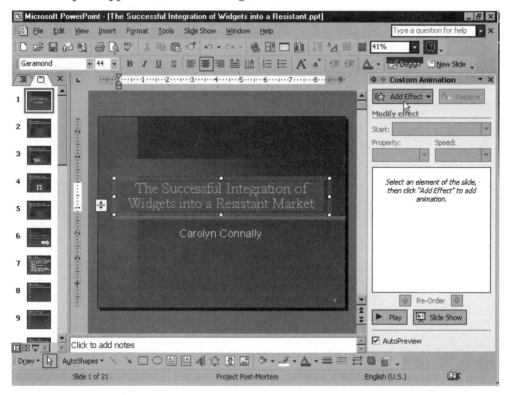

Figure 6-32 The Custom Animation pane.

2. Select a slide.

From the Preview pane to the left of your screen, click the slide to which you want to apply an Animation Scheme. The selected slide appears in the PowerPoint window.

3. Select an object.

Select a text or graphic object on your slide by clicking it.

TIP   *If you cannot select an object, it may be on your Master Slide. To apply animation to that object, you must open the Master Slide, as described above, and apply animation from there.*

4. Select an effect.

From the Add Effect menu, as shown in Figure 6-33, select whether you want the animation to provide an Entrance or an Exit, an Emphasis or a Motion Path. Then select a specific effect from the submenu.

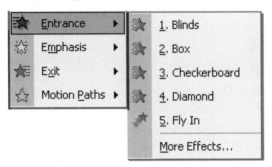

Figure 6-33   The Add Effect menu.

5. Modify the effect.

Depending upon the effect you choose, you are asked to modify the effect with your choices. For example, if you selected the Fly-In Entrance effect for the slide's title, you need to specify when the effect starts, what direction the title flies-in from, and whether you want the animation to be Very Slow, Slow, Medium, Fast, or Very Fast. To remove an effect, select the effect where it is listed in the center of the Custom Animation pane and then click the Remove button.

6. Preview your work.

Although PowerPoint demonstrates the animation effect with each setting, you can initiate all of the animations on the selected slide by clicking the Play button.

To run the entire slide show to get the full effect of your animation choices, click the Slide Show button. The slide show starts from the selected slide. If you want it to run from the beginning, select the first slide before running the show. To end a running slide show, right-click and choose End Show from the shortcut menu.

NOTE   *With some effects, Motion Path for example, the path appears on your screen. This is for your information and it does not appear in your slide show.*

Setting Slide Show Timing

If you want the presentation to run without your control, you can set timings for each slide and each effect on the slide. This is done by running the slide show and clicking when you want an effect or a transition to take place. PowerPoint times each command and saves it so that the presentation runs automatically.

1. Start timing.

Choose the Slide Show menu's Rehearse Timings command. A timing meter, showing total time elapsed for the current effect and the total for the presentation at that point, is displayed. The slide show timing begins immediately, as shown in Figure 6-34.

Figure 6-34   The Slide Show Rehearsal meter.

2. Set timings.

Run through the presentation, clicking your mouse to forward slides and effects, allowing an appropriate time for your audience to view the slides. Continue until you reach the end of the slide show. At the end of the show, right-click the screen and select End Show.

3. Accept or reject timings.

When the slide show has ended, a dialog box is displayed asking if you want to save the timings, as shown in Figure 6-35. Click Yes if you are satisfied with the settings. If you want to try it again, click No.

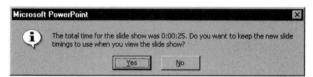

Figure 6-35   The Slide Show timings acceptance box.

When the slide show runs, it automatically progresses using the timings you set for it.

Guidelines to Effective Presentations

Although PowerPoint provides remarkable tools for building an effective presentation, using those tools is just a part of the knock-your-socks-off presentation that you want. So, we are including this section to give you some simple guidelines to keep in mind as you work with PowerPoint.

Know Your Audience

- Write your presentation for the audience you will present it to, rather than for yourself or even someone else.

- If your audience is highly conservative and/or sophisticated, leave out cute graphics and keep animation sedate.

- If your audience averages 40 to 50 years of age or even older, limit the typefaces to three at the most and use soft, complementary colors. (This has less to do with actual age, by the way, than the style that was considered acceptable when they were forming opinions.)

- If your audience is 30 or younger, use lots of action, lots of color, and a larger variety of fonts. Set items on an angle. Use unusual shapes to back text.

- If your audience is between 30 and 40, use a combination of the latter two styles.

- Keep in mind that just because you *can* do something in PowerPoint does not necessarily mean you *should* do it.

Text

- Keep presentation text short and to the point. Use only brief descriptions. Save longer explanations for your verbal accompaniment.

- Use no more than three levels of bullet points.

- Use fewer than eight bullet points per slide (three or four is actually better). If you have more information than that, separate it into additional slides.

- Use a *minimum* font size of 24 points. Larger is better.

- Use font colors that are easily read against the background color.

- Absolutely do not fill your slide up with text. Leave lots of white space (blank area) around the text so it can breathe.

Colors

- Blues and greens are soothing. Reds, oranges, and bright yellows are exciting. Consider the result you want from your presentation and choose colors accordingly.

- Use a consistent color scheme throughout.

- Consider the impact of colors on your audience. For example, red means deficit in the financial world. A presentation with red text would not come across as positive to an audience of bankers.

- Understand cultural interpretations of colors as well. Red is a color denoting good fortune in many Asian cultures, for example.

Graphics

- Avoid cute or cartoon graphics in presentations to conservative audiences.

- If a graphic denotes action, the action should move into the slide, not off of it.

- If a graphic has a face (as in a person or caricature) it should face into the slide, not off of it.

- Use graphics that augment your text, not distract from it.

- Use a consistent style of graphic throughout. In other words, do not mix cartoons with line drawings; modern styles with old-fashioned ones.

Making Your Presentation

- Smile. Let the audience know that you are glad to be there.

- Introduce yourself. Explain why you are the one making this presentation.

- Explain your objectives for the presentation.

- Speak slowly. Do not rush.

- Don't worry about making mistakes. If you know your subject, the audience will easily forgive slight mix-ups.

- Don't read the slide to your audience. Elaborate on it. Explain it. But let the audience do the reading themselves.

- Be sure to give enough time to each slide and each point on the slide for its meaning to be absorbed.

- Allow time for questions. State up-front whether you welcome questions during the presentation or want them to be held to the end.

- If you want to elicit some action from your audience, be sure to request that they do so. Call for them to take an action, make a change, work toward a goal, or otherwise follow your suggestions. A frequent mistake of presenters is to assume that the audience knows what they want them to do; therefore, they never ask for the action to take place. Always end by making an appropriate call for action.

Skill 7

USE ACCESS FOR DATA MANAGEMENT

Featuring:

- Access Terminology
- The Wonder of Wizards
- Creating a Blank Database
- Creating a Table
- Entering Data with a Form
- Analyzing Data with a Simple Query
- Publishing Your Data with an Access Report
- Sending a File to Excel
- Importing a File from Excel

Microsoft Office's Access is a highly sophisticated relational database management program. Access stores and organizes an unlimited amount of data and provides the tools you need to analyze it. Use Access to find answers, share information, and make better decisions.

If you are an experienced database user, moving to Access from another program is an easy transition. If you are new to the world of databases, you have a somewhat steeper learning curve, but this skill is here to get you started. In this skill, we discuss the essential elements of an Access database: tables, forms, queries, and reports. First, however, let's begin with some terminology.

Access Terminology

Because Access approaches database management a little differently than some database programs you may have used, we need to define some basic Access terms:

- Database—In Access, the word *database* is defined as the entire collection of data that is gathered together in one group. That means you can have several separate tables in Access, all within the same database, as well as queries and reports. As a whole, they are named and saved as a database.

- Table—A table is a collection of data on one topic, for example, Customers' Orders Table. This table may overlap with other tables, such as Customers Accounts Receivable Table or Customers Mailing List. Separating customer information out in this manner keeps tables from being unwieldy and makes analysis workable.

- Field—A field is a single data point. For example, First Name, Address, and SS# are each a field.

- Record—This is the total collection of data on one item or individual within a table. For example, the First Name, Last Name, Address, Address1, City, State, and Postal Code of a specific customer is that customer's record.

- Query—A query is a question you ask of the database. Queries can be set up to run on fields from more than one table at a time. A query is the way to determine information about the data in the database. Queries can be simple or extremely complicated. We will be dealing with simple queries in this skill. An example would be a query established to list all the customers who live within Austin, Texas.

- Form—A form is a tool that can be used to simplify data entry. Using a form to enter a record takes you step-by-step through all the fields in that record.

- Report—A report, of course, is a presentation of data arranged to provide certain information. Access reports are easily configured using the Report Wizard.

The Wonder of Wizards

More than any other program in the Office suite, Access uses wizards to create elements and tools, and to produce results. A wizard is merely a small program that produces a specific end-result after asking for information and preferences.

In Access, wizards save time by designing tables, queries, forms, and reports. All of these can be designed without the use of wizards, but wizards can save a lot of time and frustration, particularly if Access is new to you. In describing the development of Access elements and tools, we will be using the many wizards at our disposal.

Creating a Blank Database

Before you can create a table, you must create a database to store it in. To get started in Access, follow these steps:

1. Click the Blank Database link.

When you start Access, you are presented with a blank Access window and the New File pane to the right side of the window. Click the Blank Database link, as shown in Figure 7-1. The File New Database dialog box is displayed.

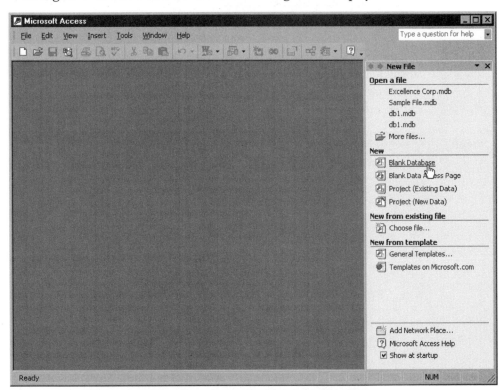

Figure 7-1   The New File pane and the Blank Database link.

2. Name the new database.

Using the directory tree in the File New Database dialog box, locate the folder in which you want to store the new database. Then name the new database and click the Create button. The Database window appears. Although blank at this time, this is where all your tables, forms, queries, and reports are stored.

NOTE *While working in Access, the Database window is shown as a separate button on your taskbar for easy activation.*

Creating a Table

While a field is the essential building block of Access, a table is the collector that holds the data together. For ease of use, an Access table should supply one essential group of information, such as Customer Contact Information. To create a new, blank table, follow these steps:

1. Start the Table Wizard.

In the Database window, click the Tables button on the Objects bar, if necessary. Then start the Table Wizard by double-clicking Create Table By Using Wizard, as shown in Figure 7-2. The first screen of the Table Wizard is displayed.

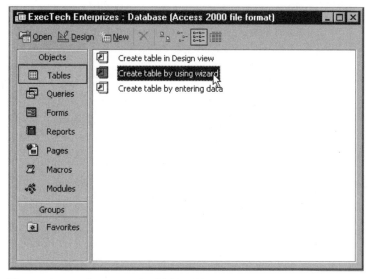

Figure 7-2   Starting the Table Wizard.

2. Select the table type.

In the first screen of the Table Wizard, choose the type of table you are going to create. Access has sample tables divided into two categories, Business and Personal. Each category provides a large number of sample tables from which to choose. Select a category and then select a table type from the Sample Tables drop-down list box, as shown in Figure 7-3.

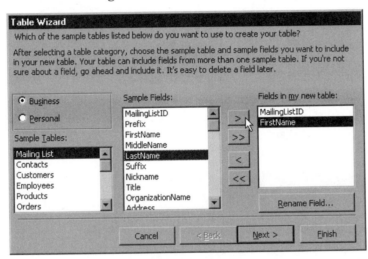

Figure 7-3   Selecting table options in the first Table Wizard screen.

3. Select table fields.

Each sample table has numerous fields typical to that kind of table. Move a field from the Sample Fields list to the Fields In My New Table list by selecting the field and clicking the top button with a right-pointing chevron. If you want to select all the fields in a sample table, click the second button with a right-pointing double chevron. Figure 7-3 shows fields being selected. It is a good idea to select the ID field in every table. This field automatically provides a unique number for each record in the table.

If you want to remove fields from your table, click the left-pointing chevron to remove selected fields and click the left-pointing double chevron to remove all fields.

If you want to rename a field (for example, PostalCode to ZipCode), move the field to the list for the new table and then click the Rename Field button. In the Rename Field dialog box that appears, enter a new name and click OK.

NOTE   *Be certain that the field you are renaming will serve in its new capacity. The sample fields are created with specific criteria (all numbers, for example, for PostalCode) so you could not use a PostalCode field for, say, Country Name. PostalCode can successfully be changed to ZipCode because they are the same thing. However, Canadian postal codes contain letters and cannot be entered in the PostalCode field as it first appears.*

Once you have completed your selection, click Next. The second Table Wizard screen is displayed.

4. Naming your table and setting the primary key.

The second Table Wizard screen allows you to name the table you are creating and set a unique field called a primary key, as shown in Figure 7-4. Just type the name in the What Do You Want To Name Your Table? text box. Then click an option button below.

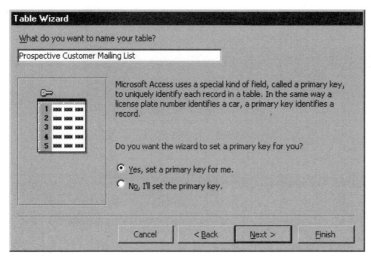

Figure 7-4   Naming your table and creating a primary key.

Until you are more familiar with Access, allowing the computer to set the primary key is a good idea. (If you have selected an ID field for your new table, it will probably serve as the primary key, because it is truly unique. With the ID field automatically generating ID numbers for records, there are never two records with the same ID.)

Click Next. The final screen of the Table Wizard is displayed.

5. Finish the wizard.

In the final screen of the Table Wizard, you are asked what you want to do next, as shown in Figure 7-5. After you are more familiar with Access, you may want to try your hand at altering a table's design but for now, we recommend that you click the Enter Data Directly Into The Table option button. (We discuss the use of forms in the next section.)

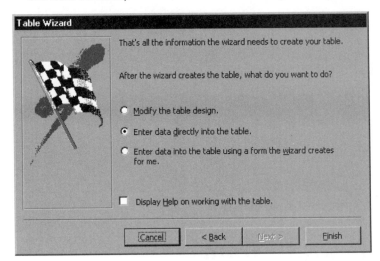

Figure 7-5   The Table Wizard final screen.

Click Finish. The wizard closes and the empty table is displayed on your screen. Only one row (for one record) is available, but once you begin that record another row is created.

6. Enter data.

All that remains is to enter data in the table. You can do this right in the table, tabbing from one field to the next, as shown in Figure 7-6. Or you can create a form.

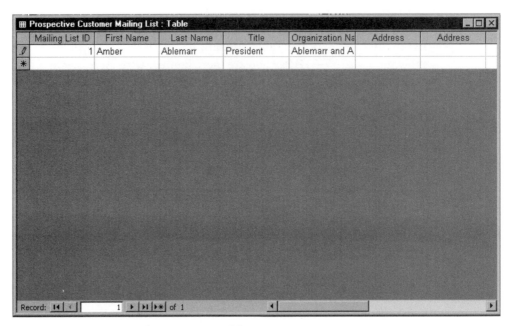

Figure 7-6   Entering data in a new table.

Entering Data with a Form

Although it is a matter of personal preference, many people feel that entering data by using a form keeps the process on track and is much easier than entering data into the table. If you find that you, too, prefer the use of a form, clicking the Enter Data Into The Table Using A Form The Computer Creates For Me option button on the final Table Wizard screen causes a form to be automatically created for you.

To enter data using a form, click in the second field (the first is the ID and is automatically filled once you begin entering data), and enter the appropriate data. Press the Tab key to move from one field to the next. When you want to begin a new record, press the Enter key.

To create a form, follow these steps:

1. **Select the form object.**

   In the Database window, click Forms on the Objects bar.

2. **Start the Form Wizard.**

   Double-click Create Form Using Wizard, as shown in Figure 7-7. The first screen of the Form Wizard is displayed.

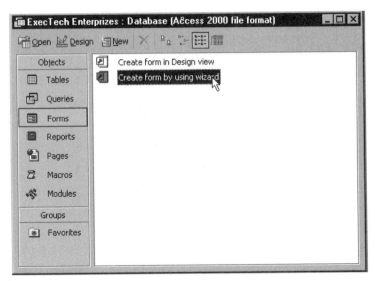

Figure 7-7   Starting the Form Wizard.

3. Select the fields.

From the Selected Fields list, select the fields that you want to appear on your form, as shown in Figure 7-8. To select all the fields, use the Move All button (with the right-pointing double chevron).

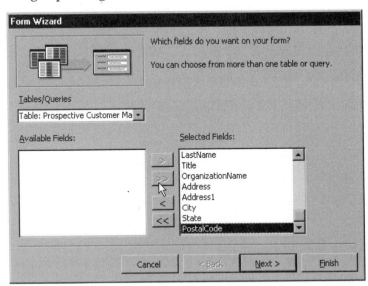

Figure 7-8   Selecting fields for the form.

When you are finished, click Next. The second Form Wizard screen is displayed.

4. Select a form layout.

This screen allows you to choose how you want your form to look. Click one of the option buttons and view the preview, as shown in Figure 7-9. When you are finished, click Next. The Form Wizard's third screen appears.

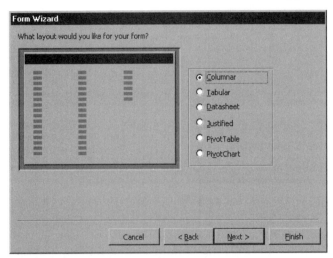

Figure 7-9 Choosing the form's layout.

5. Select a form style.

If appearance is important to you, click one of the styles and view the preview. The Standard selection creates a simple form with a gray background; the others offer some interesting backgrounds, as shown in Figure 7-10. When you are finished, click Next. The final Form Wizard screen is displayed.

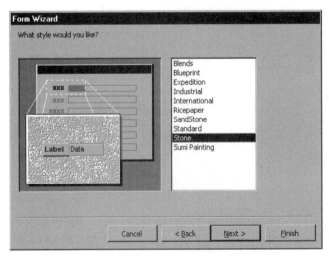

Figure 7-10 Selecting the form's style.

6. Name the form.

Enter a name for your form in the box provided, as shown in Figure 7-11. Choose a name that identifies the table for which it was created.

Figure 7-11 Entering a name for your form.

7. Finish.

Click the Open The Form To View Or Enter Information option button, and click Finish, as shown in Figure 7-12. Your new form opens. You can begin entering data, or close it until you are ready to do so.

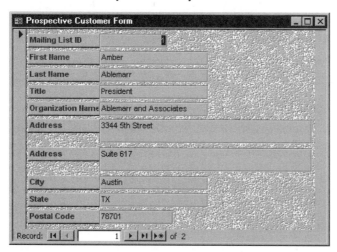

Figure 7-12 A new form ready for data entry.

Analyzing Data with a Simple Query

The purpose of a database is to store data. The purpose of a query is to retrieve that data in a fashion that provides you with information. For example, if we want to do a special mailing to our prospective customers who live in the states of Louisiana and Texas, we would design a query to run against our Prospective Customers Mailing List which would find and display those specific customers and their addresses. To do this, follow these steps:

1. **Start the Query Wizard**

   In the Database window, click Queries on the Objects bar, as shown in Figure 7-13. Then double-click Create Query By Using Wizard. The first screen of the Query Wizard is displayed.

Figure 7-13 The Database window with the Queries object selected.

2. **Select the tables or queries on which you want to base your query.**

   The first screen of the Report Wizard displays the name of a table and the fields located within that table, as shown in Figure 7-14. The Tables/Queries drop-down list box displays all tables and queries that have been created for your database. If the table name that is shown is not a table on which you are basing your query, click the drop-down arrow to display the list and select the appropriate table or query.

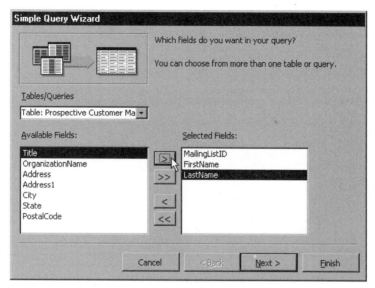

Figure 7-14 Selecting report fields.

3. Choose the fields for your query.

The fields that are contained in the selected table are displayed in the Available Fields list (see Figure 7-14). Select the fields you want shown in your completed report and move them into the Selected Fields box using the right-pointing chevron button. If you want all fields, use the button showing a right-pointing double chevron. Use the left-pointing chevron buttons to remove one field or all fields.

After your selection is complete, click Next. The next screen of the Query Wizard is displayed.

TIP   *The fields that you choose should show all the information that you need. For example, if we are pulling all records with a Texas or Louisiana address so that we can send out a mailing, we would want the query to pull just those records but show ID, FirstName, LastName, Address, Address1, City, State, and PostalCode so that we would have the names and addresses for the mailing. It is better to pull too many fields than not enough.*

4. Name the query.

In the Query Wizard's final screen, enter a name for your query in the What Title Do You Want For Your Query? text box, as shown in Figure 7-15.

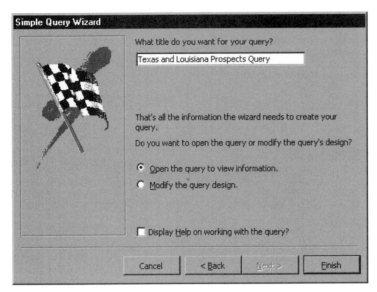

Figure 7-15 The final screen of the Query Wizard.

5. Finish the query.

Click the Open The Query To View Information option button, and click Finish. The basic query is displayed in Datasheet view, as shown in Figure 7-16.

	Mailing List ID	First Name	Last Name	Title	Organization Na	Address	Address
▶	1	Amber	Ablemarr	President	Ablemarr and A	3344 5th Street	Suite 617
	2	Betty	Biedermeyer	Regional Direct	Excellence Cor	5391 Maple Str	Building 5, Suite
	3	David	Dattwieler	CEO	The Widget Sto	23456 Main Str	
	4	Ernest	Eagleman	Account Manag	Fix-it-uppers, In	63987 Harmony	Suite 159
	5	Freida	Feinbinder		Feinbinder's	203 Central	
	6	George	Garrison	Account Manag	XYZ Corp.	4596 Symphony	
	7	Heidi	Harrison	Sales Manager	Widgets for Les	23418 Grand Pz	Suite 610
	8	Ira	Inglebrecht		Progressive, Inc	19573 Military [	Suite 1269
	9	Enrique	Bourdelon	Account Manag	Harbinger Parts	2936 Spicewood	
	10	Jenny	Jensen	Vice-President :	Heath Health Pr	5666	125th Street
	11	Karsten	Kellmann	Owner	Uptown Industri	15986 Redwood	Suite 23
	12	Noe	Hebert	Account Manag	Baton Rouge St	25698 Lightning	
	13	Lucida	Lockridge		Best's Place	12368 Uptown E	
	14	Marvin	McAllister	President	McAllister and F	1459 Overlook	Suite 652
	15	Marjorie	McGivney		Table Rock Mar	116 Station Stre	
	16	Nathan	Neighbors		Adams and Zett	459 Central Par	Suite 1259

Record: |◄| ◄ | 1 | ► | ►| | ►* | of 16

Figure 7-16 The query in Datasheet view.

NOTE   *Notice that the result is really just the original table reproduced with only the fields that you have chosen. Because we have not yet applied any criteria to the query, all records for all states are shown.*

6. Display the query in Design view.

With the query open on your screen, the Access toolbar has changed to the Query Design toolbar. Clicking the first button on that toolbar changes the view of the query from Datasheet view to Design view, as shown in Figure 7-17.

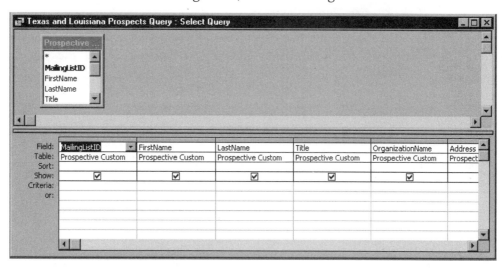

Figure 7-17 The new query in Design view.

7. Enter criteria.

In this example, we set the criteria of Texas or Louisiana. In the lower half of the Design View screen, locate the row identified as Criteria. In that row, under the State field, enter TX or LA, as shown in Figure 7-18.

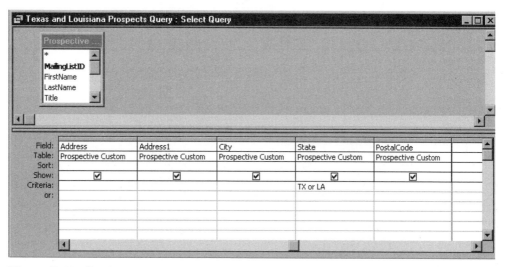

Figure 7-18 Setting query criteria.

We are using the U.S. Postal Service abbreviations because that is how the records were entered, and we are using *or* so that records from both states appear in the results. (*And* would have told Access to show any records that had both TX and LA in the State field and we would have had zero results.)

8. **Run the query against criteria.**

Located about midway on the Design Query toolbar is the Run button, shown with a large red exclamation point. Clicking the Run button runs the query against the criteria and the results show only the records we designated, Texas and Louisiana, as shown in Figure 7-19. Save your resulting query.

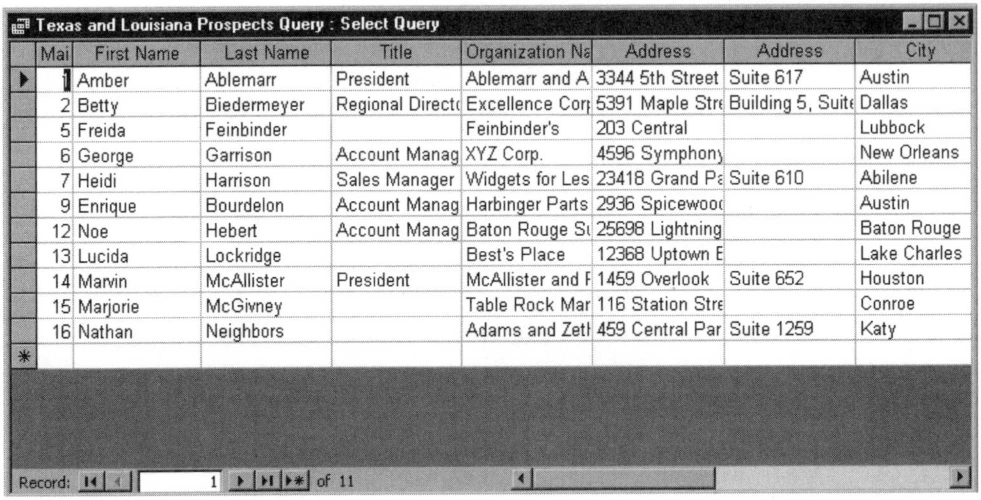

	Mai	First Name	Last Name	Title	Organization Na	Address	Address	City
▶	1	Amber	Ablemarr	President	Ablemarr and A	3344 5th Street	Suite 617	Austin
	2	Betty	Biedermeyer	Regional Directo	Excellence Corp	5391 Maple Stre	Building 5, Suite	Dallas
	5	Freida	Feinbinder		Feinbinder's	203 Central		Lubbock
	6	George	Garrison	Account Manag	XYZ Corp.	4596 Symphony		New Orleans
	7	Heidi	Harrison	Sales Manager	Widgets for Les	23418 Grand Pa	Suite 610	Abilene
	9	Enrique	Bourdelon	Account Manag	Harbinger Parts	2936 Spicewood		Austin
	12	Noe	Hebert	Account Manag	Baton Rouge Su	25698 Lightning		Baton Rouge
	13	Lucida	Lockridge		Best's Place	12368 Uptown E		Lake Charles
	14	Marvin	McAllister	President	McAllister and F	1459 Overlook	Suite 652	Houston
	15	Marjorie	McGivney		Table Rock Mar	116 Station Stre		Conroe
	16	Nathan	Neighbors		Adams and Zeth	459 Central Par	Suite 1259	Katy
*								

Record: I◄ ◄ [1] ► ►I ►* of 11

Figure 7-19 The completed query.

Publishing Your Data with an Access Report

Access offers a quick and easy way to publish your data: an Access report. A report may be based on any combination of tables and queries in your database. Additionally, Access offers several formats and styles from which to choose.

1. **Start the Report Wizard.**

In the Database window, click Reports on the Objects bar, as shown in Figure 7-20. Then double-click Create Report By Using Wizard. The first screen of the Report Wizard is displayed.

Figure 7-20 The Database window with the Reports object selected.

2. Select the tables or queries on which you want to base your report.

The first screen of the Report Wizard displays the name of a table and the fields located within that table, as shown in Figure 7-21. The Tables/Queries drop-down list box displays all tables and queries that have been created for your database. If the table name that is shown is not a table or query on which you are basing your report, click the drop-down arrow to display the list and select the appropriate table or query.

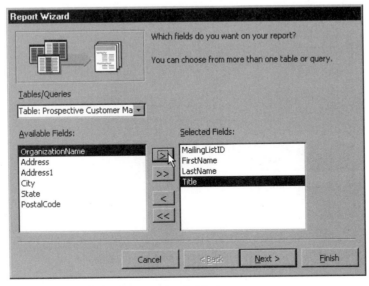

Figure 7-21 Selecting report fields.

3. Choose the fields for your report.

The fields that are contained in the selected table are displayed in the Available Fields list (see Figure 7-21). Select the fields you want shown in your completed report and move them into the Selected Fields area using the right-pointing chevron button. If you want all fields, use the button showing a right-pointing double chevron. Use the left-pointing chevron buttons to remove one field or all fields.

You can pull fields from other tables or queries as well. Simply select a new table or query from the Tables/Queries list and move the desired fields into the Selected Fields box.

After your selection is complete, click Next. The next screen of the Report Wizard is displayed.

4. Select grouping and set priorities.

On the second screen of the Report Wizard, you are given the opportunity to re-arrange the fields into the order you want and to set priorities, as shown in Figure 7-22. Because our data is already in a usable form for a mailing list, we won't make any changes here. Click Next to display the third Report Wizard screen.

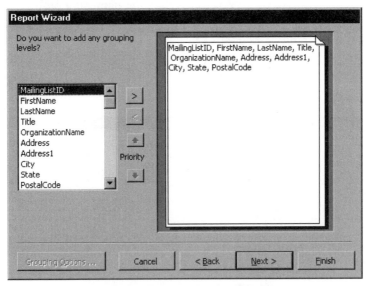

Figure 7-22 Establishing field order and priority.

5. Set sorting order.

In the finished report, you want your data organized so that all records in each state are together, as well as cities and zip codes. We want to establish the sort keys so that the finished report is organized.

In the third Report Wizard screen, click the drop-down arrow for the first sort key box. In that list, all fields in the report are listed. We want the records sorted by State so that is the sort we selected. In the following three sort key boxes, we chose City, PostalCode, and LastName, respectively, as shown in Figure 7-23. Then click Next to display the fourth Report Wizard screen.

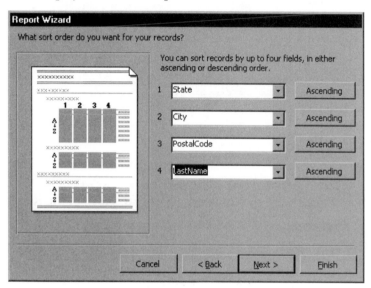

Figure 7-23 Setting the sort keys.

6. Select report layout.

The fourth Report Wizard screen offers you the opportunity to select the layout for your report, as shown in Figure 7-24. When you select a layout on the right, the preview is shown on the left. When you are finished, click Next.

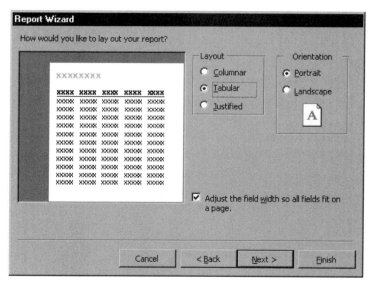

Figure 7-24 Selecting a report layout.

7. Select a report style.

You select a report style in the fifth screen of the Report Wizard. Click one of the choices on the right to see the preview on the left, as shown in Figure 7-25. When your selection is made, click Next to reveal the final screen of the Report Wizard.

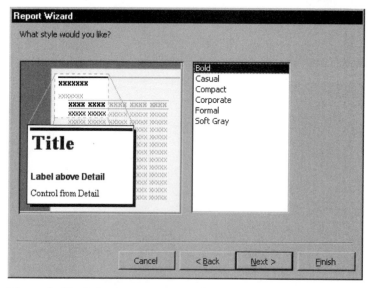

Figure 7-25 Selecting a report style.

8. Name the report.

In the final screen of the Report Wizard, enter the name you want for your report, as shown in Figure 7-26.

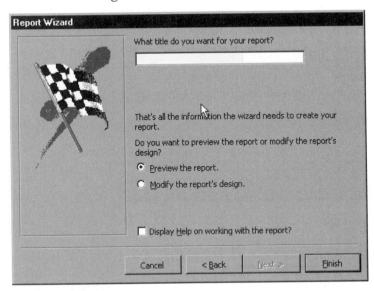

Figure 7-26 Finishing the report.

Click the Preview The Report option button, and click Finish. Your completed report appears, as shown in Figure 7-27.

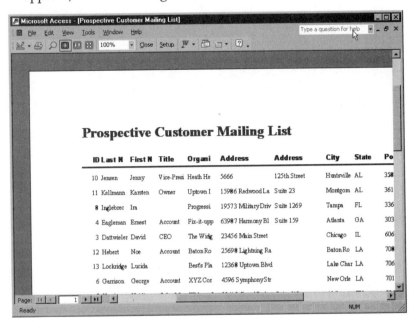

Figure 7-27 The completed report.

Sending a File to Excel

Although there is a vast difference in the purpose of Microsoft Excel and Access, there may be times when you want to move an Access table to Excel for use in a spreadsheet. The process of doing so is simple. Follow these steps:

1. Select a table to export to Excel.

In the Database window, click Tables on the Objects bar and select the table that you want to send to Excel, as shown in Figure 7-28.

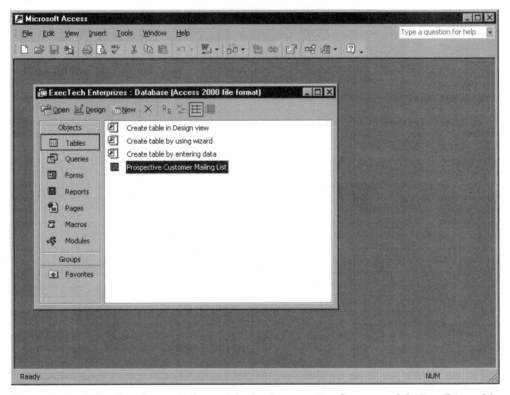

Figure 7-28 The Database window with the Prospective Customer Mailing List table selected.

2. Open the Export Table dialog box.

Choose the File menu's Export command. The Export Table dialog box appears.

3. Select a version of Excel.

In the Export Table dialog box, click the drop-down arrow next to the Save As Type box, as shown in Figure 7-29, and select the version of Excel to which you want to send the file.

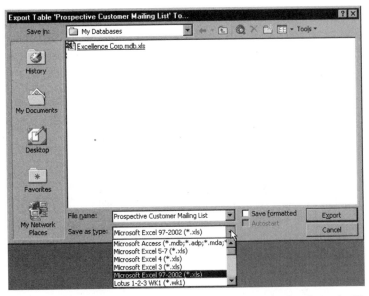

Figure 7-29 The Export Table dialog box with the Save As Type list displayed.

4. Save the file.

Using the list in the Export Table dialog box, locate the folder where you want to store the table as an Excel file. Then click the Export button.

After the Export process is complete, a copy of the table is saved in the new location as an Excel file. The original table remains in your Access database.

Importing a File from Excel

You may occasionally want to copy a file from Excel and place it into an Access database. To do this, follow these steps:

1. Open the Import dialog box.

In the Database window, choose the File menu's Get External Data command and then choose Import. The Import dialog box opens.

2. Import an Excel file.

Set the Files Of Type to Microsoft Excel. Using the list in the Import dialog box, locate the Excel file you want to import into Access. Click the Import button. The Import Wizard is displayed.

3. Select worksheet or named ranges to import.

The Import Spreadsheet Wizard helps you select and configure the Excel file you want to import. If you have more than one worksheet in the workbook selected, you need to tell Access which worksheet it is. Or, if you have named ranges within the selected workbook, you can select one of the named ranges for import, as shown in Figure 7-30. Select the appropriate worksheet or file, and click Next.

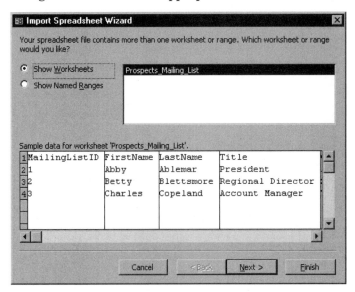

Figure 7-30 Selecting a worksheet for import.

4. Identify column headings.

If the first row of the Excel range contains column headings, select the First Row Contains Column Headings check box. Click Next to proceed.

5. Enter storage criteria.

The third screen of the Import Spreadsheet Wizard asks whether you want to import the Excel range as a new table or place the data in an existing table, as shown in Figure 7-31. If you choose to place it in an existing table, tell Access which table to place it in.

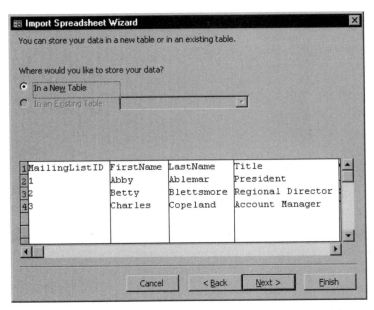

Figure 7-31 Making the selection to import as a new table.

Then click Next to display the fourth Import Spreadsheet Wizard screen.

6. Configure fields for new table.

In the fourth screen of the Import Spreadsheet Wizard, select each field, one by one, and rename it (if you want) and indicate whether it is okay for the field to contain duplicates, as shown in Figure 7-32. In our scenario of the Prospective Customer Mailing List, the one field that should not have duplicates is the ID field. All others could possibly have duplication. If you do not want a field in the Excel range to appear in your Access table, select the Do Not Import Field (Skip) check box. When you are finished, click Next.

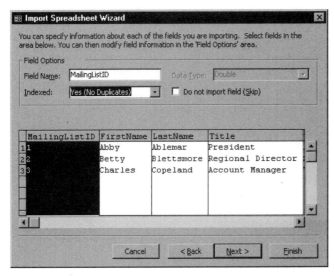

Figure 7-32 Configuring fields.

7. Set the primary key.

The fifth screen of the Import Spreadsheet Wizard allows you to set the primary key or allows Access to add a field to be used as the primary key, as shown in Figure 7-33. Since we already have an ID field, we can use it as the primary key. Therefore, we would click the Choose My Own Primary Key option button. However, if you are importing a table from Excel that does not contain a unique field, allow Access to add that field. Click Next. The final Import Spreadsheet Wizard screen is displayed.

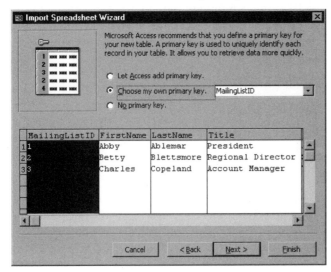

Figure 7-33 Setting the primary key.

8. Finish the import.

Give the new Access table a name by entering it in the Import To Table text box. Then click Finish. A copy of the Excel range has been placed in Access as a new table, as shown in Figure 7-34.

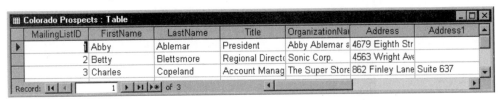

	MailingListID	FirstName	LastName	Title	OrganizationNa	Address	Address1
▶	1	Abby	Ablemar	President	Abby Ablemar a	4679 Eighth Str	
	2	Betty	Blettsmore	Regional Direct	Sonic Corp.	4563 Wright Ave	
	3	Charles	Copeland	Account Manag	The Super Store	862 Finley Lane	Suite 637

Figure 7-34 The newly created table.

Appendix A

USE OBJECT LINKING AND EMBEDDING

Featuring:

- OLE Terminology
- Inserting a Linked Object into a Document
- Embedding an Object in a Document

Although not part of routine Microsoft Office usage, Object Linking and Embedding (OLE) is included here because it is a powerful technique that can make life easier, particularly for the business user. This process creates connections between documents that provide automatic updating and ease of editing.

What would OLE do for you? Let's look at a likely example:

You have a Microsoft PowerPoint presentation that you use on a regular basis. Even though you use the same presentation over and over again, the data must be updated regularly to reflect current sales figures that are reworked weekly in Microsoft Excel. One such update in the PowerPoint document is a chart based on the weekly Excel figures. You would like to make the updates simpler.

Using Office's Object Linking feature makes the updates automatic. Create the chart in Excel based on the market pricing figures. Then copy it and paste it into the presentation using OLE techniques so that a *link* is established between the copy in PowerPoint and the original in Excel. Then whenever the source data is edited in Excel, the Excel chart is updated and the linked chart in PowerPoint is updated as well.

Using the same example, if you *embedded* the chart, then the connection is to the source application, Excel, rather than the original chart. In this case, to edit the chart, you would double-click the chart and Excel would open within the PowerPoint slide for you to use Excel techniques to make changes.

OLE Terminology

Once you understand the concept, OLE is a very simple (and useful) process. But in order to explain the concept, we need to take a look at the following OLE terminology:

- Object—An object is any element of a document, spreadsheet, slide or database. Text, worksheet cells, and graphics are all objects. From the perspective of OLE, an object is data placed in a document from another document or application.

- Link—A link is a connection between an object and its source document.

- Embed—Embedding establishes a connection between an object and the application that was used to create it in its source document.

- Source application—The source application is the program that was originally used to create an object.

- Source document—The source document is the file in which a linked or embedded object was originally created.

- Source data—The source data is the object that is copied in the source document and pasted into the destination document.

- Destination document—This is the document into which objects are pasted using linking or embedding techniques.

Inserting a Linked Object into a Document

To establish a link between an object and its source document, follow these steps:

1. Copy the object.

In the source document, select the object and copy it to the Clipboard by clicking the Copy button on the Standard toolbar or choosing the Edit menu's Copy command, as shown in Figure A-1.

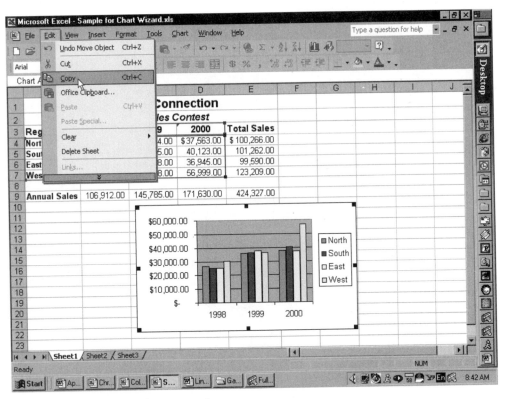

Figure A-1   Copying the source data.

2. Place an insertion point in the destination document where you want the object to appear.

The new, or destination, document can be already open, but it is not necessary. You can even create the document at this point if you want. Once the destination document is open, place your insertion point where you want the linked object to appear.

3. Use the Paste Special command.

Choose the Edit menu's Paste Special command, as shown in Figure A-2. The Paste Special dialog box appears.

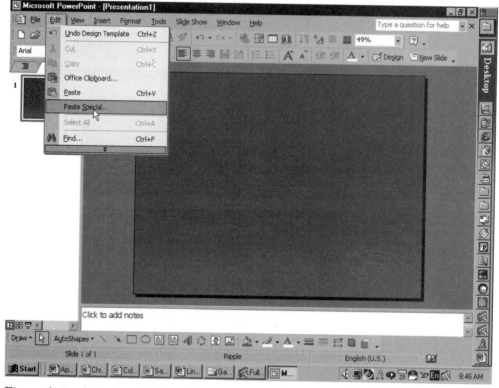

Figure A-2 Selecting the Paste Special command.

4. Paste the object into the destination document.

Click the Paste Link option button, and in the As drop-down list box, select the item that identifies the data as an object, as shown in Figure A-3. Click OK.

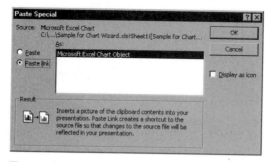

Figure A-3 The Paste Special dialog box specifying a linked object.

5. Update data as appropriate.

If the source data is changed, open the destination document, right-click the object, and choose Update Link from the shortcut menu, as shown in Figure A-4. The pasted data reflects the information as it is in the source document.

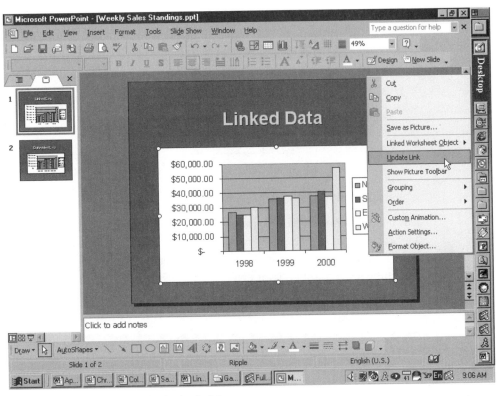

Figure A-4 Updating the linked object.

Embedding an Object in a Document

To embed an object in a destination document, follow these steps:

1. Copy the object.

In the source document, select the object and copy it to the Clipboard by clicking the Copy button on the Standard toolbar or choosing the Edit menu's Copy command.

2. Place an insertion point in the destination document where you want the object to appear.

The new, or destination, document can be already open, but it is not necessary. You can even create the document at this point if you want. Once the destination document is open, place your insertion point where you want the linked object to appear.

3. Using Paste Special, paste the object into the destination document.

Choose the Edit menu's Paste Special command. The Paste Special dialog box appears. Click the Paste option button, and in the As drop-down list box, select the item that identifies the data as an object, as shown in Figure A-5. Click OK.

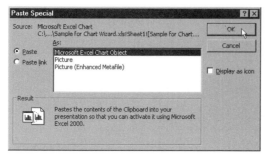

Figure A-5   The Paste Special dialog box specifying an embedded object.

4. Update as needed.

If you need to make changes to your embedded object, double-click the object. The application that was used to create the object originally opens within the destination document, complete with toolbars, so that you may use the power of the original application to make your changes, as shown in Figure A-6. Once changes are complete, click anywhere on the document away from the object. The source application closes and returns the destination document to its original format.

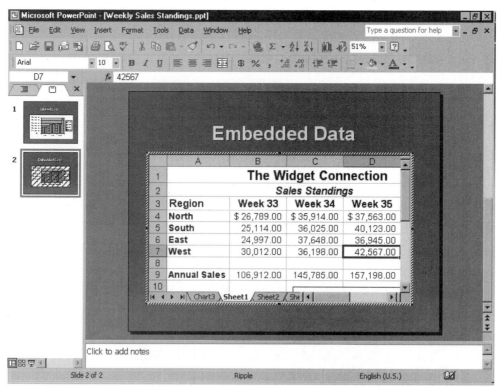

Figure A-6   Updating an embedded chart using the source application within PowerPoint.

Appendix B

USING THIS BOOK WITH OFFICE 2000

Featuring:

- Skill 1: Use Common Office Tools
- Skill 2: Manage Files
- Skill 4: Use Word for Document Generation
- Skill 5: Use Excel for Spreadsheet Functions
- Skill 6: Use PowerPoint for Powerful Presentations
- Skill 7: Use Access for Data Management

This appendix is for those who have the earlier version of Microsoft Office, Office 2000. It may be that you bought this book because you expect to upgrade to the latest version of Office in the future. Or perhaps you want to see the differences between the older Office 2000 and the new Office XP before you purchase the upgrade software. Whatever the situation, this section is provided to give information on Office 2000 where it differs from the newest version discussed in the body of this book.

Skill 1: Use Common Office Tools

Although there are many visual differences between the way Office XP and Office 2000 look as you are using them, essentially they work much the same.

Using Help Without the Office Assistant

The Help feature of Office has come a long way since the early days of computers when you almost had to be a computer expert just to read the Help files. There is only one difference in using Help in Office 2000, as shown in Figure B-1, and the newer version discussed in Skill 1.

- Office 2000 does not have an Answer Wizard box on the menu bar in which you can type a question.

The Answer Wizard is present in Office 2000, but you must activate the Office Assistant or open the Help window to utilize it.

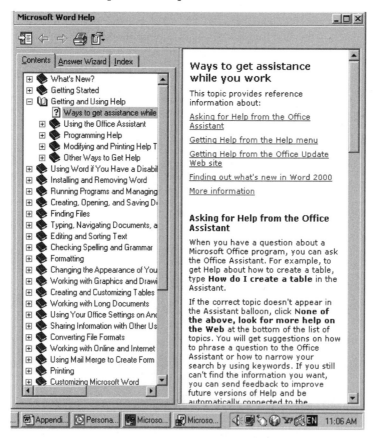

Figure B-1   The Help window in Word 2000.

The Clipboard

The Clipboard just keeps getting better and better. In Office 2000 the Clipboard works essentially the same as the new version described in Skill 1. There are, however, two distinct differences.

- Using the Clipboard in Office 2000 opens a Clipboard toolbar rather than the Clipboard pane.

  When you cut or paste two or more objects to the Clipboard, the Clipboard toolbar appears on your screen, as shown in Figure B-2, or it may be opened by right-clicking any toolbar and selecting the Clipboard option from the shortcut menu, as shown in Figure B-3.

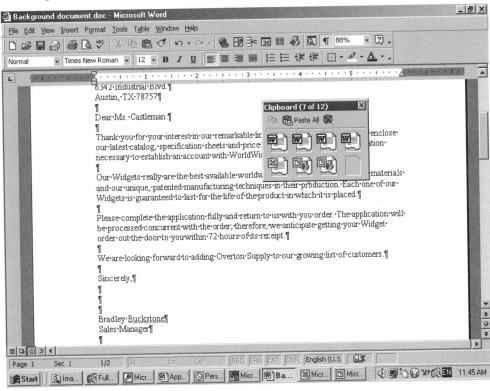

Figure B-2   The Clipboard toolbar containing seven objects.

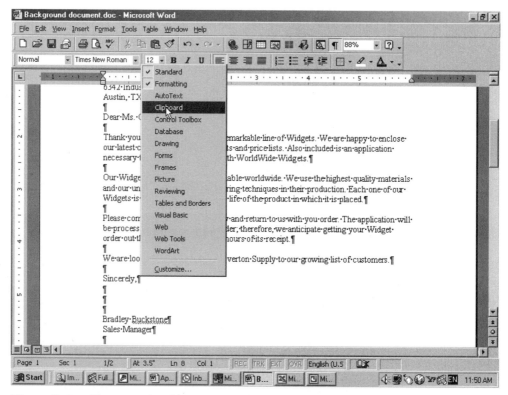

Figure B-3 Choosing the Clipboard toolbar from the Toolbars shortcut menu.

- In Office 2000, the Clipboard has a maximum capacity of 12 objects, rather than 24.

For those of us accustomed to the Clipboard holding only *one* image, this is still a great step forward.

To paste the last object cut or copied to the Clipboard, simply click the Paste button on the Standard toolbar (or choose the Edit menu's Paste command). To choose from the other 11 possible objects on the Clipboard, click the appropriate object on the Clipboard toolbar and the object appears at the location of the insertion point.

Skill 2: Manage Files

Most of the differences in file management between Office 2000 and those described in Skill 2 are only visual. Office 2000 does not display panes to the right or left of the document area; instead, choices are made from dialog boxes that appear on your screen as appropriate.

Creating a New File

Whether creating a new file from a button on the Standard toolbar or from the File menu's New command, Office 2000 provides you with dialog boxes for you to make your selections.

Creating a New File from the Standard Toolbar

Clicking the New button on the Standard toolbar in Office 2000 provides an identical result to that described in Skill 2 in all of the applications, except for PowerPoint. The only difference is in the way in which the choices are offered to you.

- Clicking the New button on the Standard toolbar in PowerPoint 2000 opens the New Slide dialog box.

  Select a slide format from the New Slide dialog box, as shown in Figure B-4, and click OK. A new presentation opens containing one slide, based on your choice.

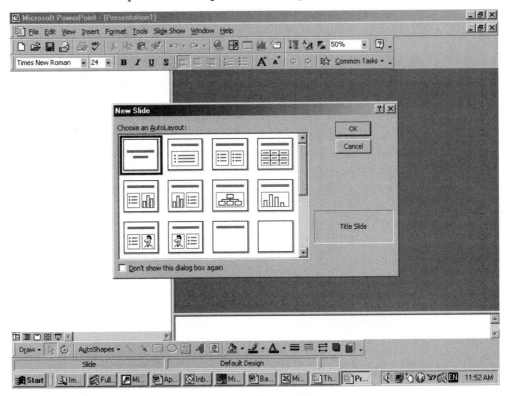

Figure B-4 The New Slide dialog box in PowerPoint.

Creating a New Document from the File Menu

Using the File menu's New command offers you more choices in the type of file you can create. Again, the difference between Office 2000 and the new version, as described in Skill 2, is mostly visual.

- Choosing the File menu's New command in Office 2000 displays the New dialog box for you to select the kind of file you want to create.

  Depending upon the application, the New dialog box offers choices of templates, wizards, or predesigned documents from which to choose. Double-clicking your selection or selecting and clicking OK opens the new document on your screen.

Using AutoRecover

AutoRecover is a feature found in Word and PowerPoint, and it is an indispensable aid in recovering documents that have been jeopardized by sudden power outages or other unplanned system shutdowns. In Office 2000 it works like it does in the new version discussed in Skill 2, but like many other processes discussed here, it looks very different.

- When your computer is restarted or the application is reopened following an unplanned shut down, AutoRecover reopens any Word or PowerPoint documents that were open at the time of shut down.

  The recovered document opens automatically, as shown in Figure B-5, with (Recovered) in the title bar. There is no pane to the left nor are there any choices to make. Just as in the newer version, the recovered document is an unnamed file and is recovered from the last AutoRecover save. You should save the recovered file under the document's name.

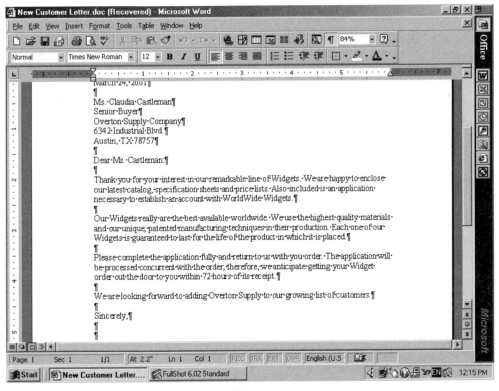

Figure B-5   A recovered document in Word 2000.

Enabling AutoRecover and setting AutoRecover intervals is performed identically to that discussed in Skill 2.

Opening an Existing File

For the most part, you open an existing file in Office 2000 just as you do in the newer version of Office. There is one slight exception.

- The Recently Used Files list appears at the bottom of the File menu only; it does not appear in a task pane.

Enabling the Recently Used Files list and setting the number of files to be shown is done identically to the discussion in Skill 2.

Skill 4: Use Word for Document Generation

Except for the file management differences discussed above in this appendix, Microsoft Word 2000 works essentially like it's newer version. Such differences are largely in appearance. However, there is one major exception.

Entering Text Using Speech Recognition

The Speech Recognition feature discussed in Skill 4 is a major software advancement for Word or any word-processing program.

• Word 2000 does not have the Speech Recognition feature.

Skill 5: Use Excel for Spreadsheet Functions

Just like Word, discussed above, there are few essential differences in the way Excel 2000 works and the newer version discussed in Skill 5. If you can use Excel in one version, you probably can use it in another. This section provides information on the differences in the appearances of the two program versions.

Entering Data

Enter data into an Excel 2000 spreadsheet just as you would in the new version discussed in Skill 5. However, the look of two of the screens is different in Excel 2000.

Functions

Functions work the same in Excel 2000 as they do in the new version of the program. Although the appearance of the wizard used to locate and insert the correct function is different, the process is essentially the same.

• Excel 2000 uses the Paste Function dialog box to locate and insert the appropriate function.

Clicking the Paste Function button (identified by *fx*) on the Standard toolbar opens the Paste Function dialog box, as shown in Figure B-6. This Excel 2000 dialog box is used exactly like the Insert Function dialog box in the newer application.

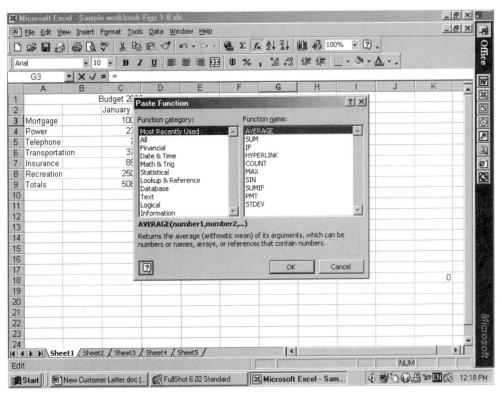

Figure B-6   The Paste Function dialog box.

After selecting the appropriate function, click OK. The Function Arguments box opens attached to the formula bar.

Enter the arguments in the appropriate boxes, or identify the correct data by clicking the Collapse/Expand button to the right of the argument box, as shown in Figure B-7, and selecting the data, as shown in Figure B-8, just as discussed in the section on the Insert Function dialog box in Skill 5.

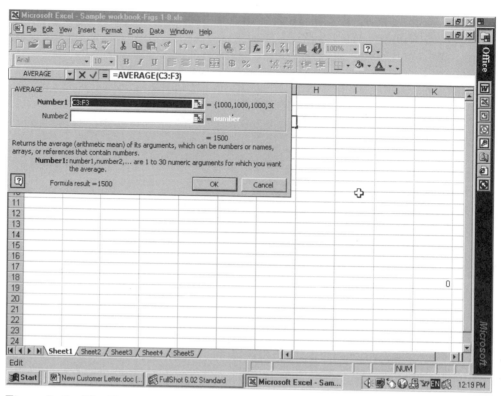

Figure B-7 The Function Arguments dialog box attached to the formula bar.

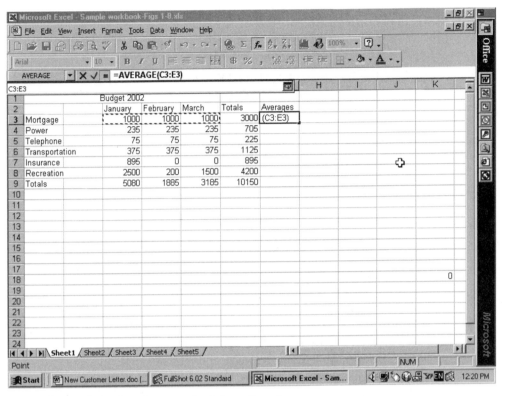

Figure B-8   Selecting data required for a function.

After entering the arguments, click OK. The function is entered into your worksheet.

Formatting Data and Worksheets

There is only one difference in Excel 2000 formatting from that discussed in Skill 5.

Special Pasting Options

The special pasting options offered in the newest program are a new innovation for Excel.

- The special pasting options are not available in Excel 2000.

Although the Paste Special command exists in Excel 2000, it performs a different function from that in the newer software.

Skill 6: Use PowerPoint for Powerful Presentations

PowerPoint has been a workhorse program since it's earliest versions. PowerPoint 2000 and the new version are not exceptions. Understanding and utilizing the features of PowerPoint provides you with the ability to impress, persuade, and inform clients, corporate executives, and the public in a professional, sophisticated manner. Just as in the discussions above, the differences between PowerPoint 2000 and its most recent counterpart are largely visual.

PowerPoint Terminology

PowerPoint terminology changes little between the two versions; however, there is a distinct difference in the screen layout between the two, making it necessary to redefine some of the PowerPoint views for users of PowerPoint 2000.

Defining PowerPoint Views

If you compare the appearance of the views discussed below with those in Skill 6, you see a change.

- Normal view—The Normal view of PowerPoint 2000 has the Outline pane to the left of the slide as discussed in Skill 6. However, there is no Slides tab.

  The Normal view, as shown in Figure B-9, presents the slide as well as the outline on which the presentation is based. It is the slide that is selected in the Outline pane that appears to the right. Text may be edited either in the Outline pane or directly on the slide. The Normal view can be accessed from the View menu or by clicking the Normal View button on the status bar.

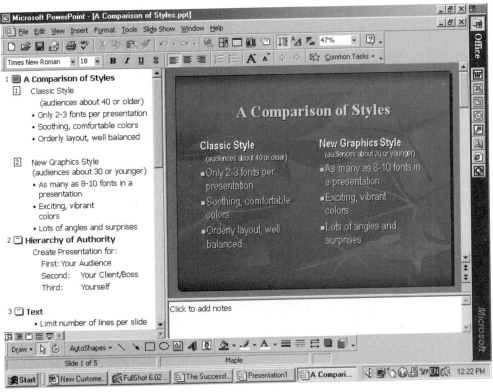

Figure B-9   The Normal view in PowerPoint 2000.

- Slide view—The Slide view presents the active slide with only a small pane to the left for selecting the slide to display.

A nearly full-screen presentation of the active slide is seen in PowerPoint 2000's Slide view, as shown in Figure B-10. This view is accessible only by clicking the Slide View button on the left side of the status bar.

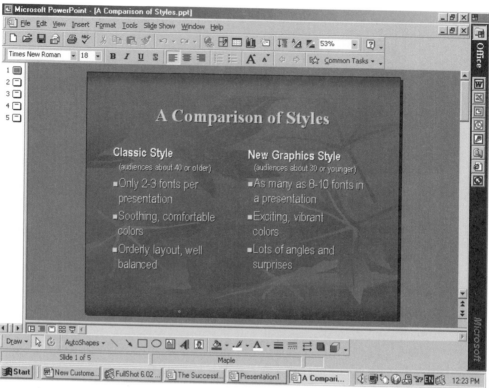

Figure B-10 Slide view in PowerPoint 2000.

Enhancing Your Presentation

Basically, the real power of PowerPoint lies in the ways in which you can enhance the words that appear on each slide through layout, clip art, and animation. PowerPoint 2000 contains most of the enhancement features of the newer version but using some of those features requires a different set of steps.

Applying a Design Template

The design of the presentation is what gives it personality. PowerPoint 2000, like its successor, comes with many design templates coordinated by theme and color to provide that extra punch. However, the process is slightly different in PowerPoint 2000.

- Open the Apply Design Template dialog box by choosing the Format menu's Apply Design Template command.

  The Apply Design Template dialog box, shown in Figure B-11, provides a list of the design templates available (on the left) as well as a preview (on the right) of the layout selected. After you have made your choice, click Apply, and the design is applied to your active presentation.

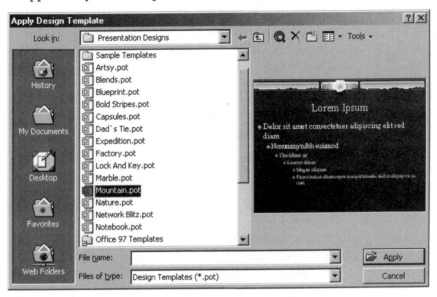

Figure B-11 The Apply Design Template dialog box.

Adding Clip Art

Where would a presentation be without clip art? PowerPoint 2000 comes with a large amount of clip art built into the program. Accessing that clip art requires a slightly different approach.

- Insert clip art using the Insert ClipArt dialog box.

  Open the Insert ClipArt dialog box by choosing the Insert menu's Picture command. Then choose Clip Art. The dialog box opens, as shown in Figure B-12, displaying tabs for pictures, sounds, and motion clips. Click the appropriate tab, select a category, and click the clip art of your choice. The object is inserted into your presentation and can be sized using the techniques described in Skill 6.

Figure B-12 The Insert ClipArt dialog box.

Using Mini Applications to Add Objects

As discussed in Skill 6, PowerPoint comes with several mini applications that insert specific objects such as stylized text, charts, and organizational charts into your presentations. All of the mini applications discussed in Skill 6 appear in PowerPoint 2000 with one exception.

- The Diagram mini application is not available in PowerPoint 2000.

  The Diagram feature is new in the latest version of PowerPoint and, therefore, does not appear in PowerPoint 2000. One of the diagram formats, Organization Chart, however, is available from the Insert menu's Picture command. Just choose Organization Chart from the Clip Art menu.

Polishing Your Slide Show

If you are using PowerPoint to create an onscreen presentation, you can add special effects to make a "Wow!" impression. As with so many of the features in the new Office application, these effects work essentially the same in PowerPoint 2000; they just look different.

Adding Transitions

As mentioned in Skill 6, a transition is the way one slide leads into another. The newer version of PowerPoint has more transitions than the older software; however, PowerPoint 2000 has many transition schemes to choose from. The process of applying a transition is slightly different.

- To apply a transition to a slide, use the Slide Transition dialog box.

Applying transitions from the Slide Sorter view makes it convenient to select first one slide and then another. Select a slide, and then choose the Slide Show menu's Slide Transition command. The Slide Transition dialog box opens, as shown in Figure B-13. Select the transition type from the box under the picture. Then select the speed at which you want the transition to take place by clicking one of the three option buttons.

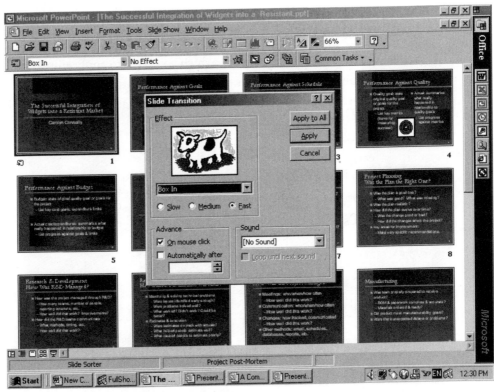

Figure B-13 The Slide Transition dialog box.

Choose whether you want the transition to take place upon a mouse click or to advance automatically after the number of seconds you set in the accompanying spin box.

You may also select a sound to accompany a transition.

When your choices are completed, click Apply to place the transition on that one slide, or click Apply To All to place the same transition on all slides.

Adding PowerPoint Animation

PowerPoint animation adds really cool effects to your presentation. Although the animations found in PowerPoint 2000 are very good, there are less of them than are in the newer program. Additionally, applying animations in PowerPoint 2000 uses a dialog box rather than a task pane.

• Apply custom animation to your PowerPoint 2000 presentation using the Custom Animation dialog box.

In the Slide view, display the slide to which you want to apply animation. Select the object to be animated, and then open the Custom Animation dialog box by choosing the Slide Show menu's Custom Animation command. Configure the object's animation through the following settings:

1. Use the Effects tab, as shown in Figure B-14.

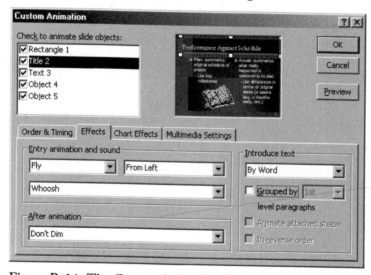

Figure B-14 The Custom Animation dialog box showing the Effects tab.

Check To Animate Slide Objects—By clicking in the selection box next to the slide's objects, you apply animation to specific objects. If you are unsure which object is which, click the object name and the object is selected in the preview to the right.

Entry Animation And Sound—Select the type of entry animation you want by selecting it from the first drop-down list box. In the box to the right, select from where you want the animation to originate. If you want to add sounds to the animation, select a sound from the list box across the bottom of the section.

After Animation—You can select an effect for the object after the animation has been completed. Selecting a color changes the object to that color. Selecting one of the Hide commands causes the object to disappear immediately after animation or after the next mouse click.

Introduce Text—If the object you are animating is text, select whether it enters the slide All At Once, By Word, or By Letter; by paragraph level, or in reverse order.

2. Use the Order & Timing tab, as shown in Figure B-15.

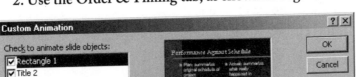

Figure B-15 The Custom Animation dialog box showing the Order & Timing tab.

Animation Order—Use this field to determine which animation effects occur in what order. Select one of the animated objects, and use the Move buttons to move the object up or down on the list.

Start Animation—Using the option buttons, select whether the animation is triggered by a mouse click or begins automatically, after the number of seconds you set in the spin box, following the previous event.

Click the Preview button to see the effect of animation on the slide.

After making all your selections, click OK to apply the animations to your slide.

Skill 7: Use Access for Data Management

The functions of Access are consistent between the two versions with the exception that Access 2000 uses dialog boxes instead of task panes.

Creating a Blank Database

Instead of using the task pane to create a blank database, Access 2000 uses the New dialog box.

- Use the New dialog box to provide a blank database in which to create tables, forms, queries, and reports.

Open the New dialog box in Access 2000, as shown in Figure B-16, by clicking the New button on the Standard toolbar and selecting Database. Then click OK. After naming it, the new database appears in the Access 2000 window.

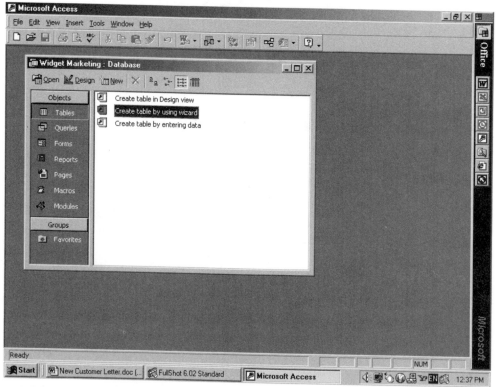

Figure B-16 A new blank database.

GLOSSARY

animation

In a PowerPoint onscreen presentation, animation is movement caused by an **object** entering a **slide** or following a path around the screen.

Answer Wizard

The Answer Wizard uses a natural language interface to locate Help topics in response to a typed question.

AutoContent Wizard

The AutoContent Wizard is a convenient mini program that does most of the work in the development of a **presentation**.

AutoCorrect

AutoCorrect automatically corrects typical misspellings and typos. AutoCorrect's **database** contains hundreds of typical errors and more can be added as needed.

AutoFill

In Excel, AutoFill is a feature that allows you to continue a pattern by dragging on the AutoFill handle. For example, you can AutoFill days of the week, months, numbers with a specific interval, or custom lists.

AutoFormat

AutoFormat is a feature within Word and Excel that automatically formats an **object** or a document according to preset criteria.

AutoRecover

AutoRecover is a feature of Word and PowerPoint that provides extra insurance against losing data because of a sudden power outage or unexpected computer shut down. When active, AutoRecover periodically saves a temporary copy of your file.

AutoText

AutoText allows you to save text blocks of any size and easily insert them as needed into a **document**.

cell

In Excel, a cell is the box formed by the intersection of a **column** and a **row**. Cells are identified by the column's letter and the row's number.

clip art

Clip art is graphic images that can be added to a **document** or a **presentation** to provide visual enhancement.

Clipboard

The Clipboard is a memory buffer that holds as many as 24 **objects** that have been **cut** or **copied** so that you can **paste** them into a new location.

column

In Excel, a column is an element of a **worksheet** that runs vertically through the length of the sheet and is identified by letters of the alphabet.

copy

Copying an **object** means that you leave it where it is in a **document** while placing a copy of it on the **Clipboard** so that you can **paste** it into additional locations.

cut

To cut an **object** means that you are removing the object from its location and placing it on the **Clipboard** so that it may be **pasted** elsewhere. In effect, you move the object.

database

In Access, the word *database* is defined as the entire collection of data that is gathered together in one group.

dialog box

A dialog box is a window that asks for instructions or preferences. In other words, it allows you to carry on a dialogue with the program.

document

The processed and formatted information generated by any Office program is a document. It may also be called a file.

document orientation

A document's orientation is the way the text is positioned on the page for reading. Portrait orientation means that the page is in a vertical position while being read, as in a standard business letter. Landscape orientation puts the paper in a horizontal position, perhaps to accommodate wide tables or illustrations.

e-mail

E-mail is electronic mail; a message sent electronically, over the Internet, from one computer to another.

field

A field is a single data point. For example, First Name, Address, and SS# are each a field.

form

A form is a tool that facilitates data entry by taking you step by step through all of the **fields** in that **record**.

Formatting toolbar

The Formatting toolbar contains buttons and menus that provide formatting of a **document** created by the application.

formula

A formula is the instruction given to Excel as to how a number or group of numbers should be manipulated.

formula bar

The formula bar is the part of an Excel **worksheet** that displays the data entered in a worksheet.

function

A function is a prebuilt **formula.** It accepts input **values,** or arguments, and then makes a calculation and returns a result.

label

In Excel, a label is any information entered in a **worksheet** that you don't want to manipulate arithmetically. Labels are frequently composed of text rather than numbers. Any data entry that contains even one text character creates a label.

Master Slide

The Master Slide contains the plan for how your **slides** look. Any text or graphic that is placed on the Master Slide, by default, is shown on all slides in a **presentation.**

Media Gallery

In PowerPoint, the Media Gallery stores and organizes the **clip art,** photographs, videos, and sounds that come with or are added later to the PowerPoint software.

Name box

The Name box is the part of an Excel **worksheet** that shows the **cell** reference of a selected cell or the name of the cell or range of cells if a name has been created for it.

object

An object is any graphic, text, spreadsheet **cell** or range of cells, or other **document** element that can be selected by the mouse.Office Assistant

The Office Assistant is a cartoon character that serves as an interface to the Office Help **database.**

Office Assistant

The Office Assistant is a cartoon character that serves as an interface to the Office Help **database.**

Office shortcut bar

The Office shortcut bar provides rapid, one-click access to the Office applications or, upon customization, any program or **document** on your computer.

Outlook Shortcuts bar

The Outlook Shortcuts bar is a toolbar that runs vertically on the left side of the Outlook document area. The Outlook Shortcuts bar contains buttons for the Outlook features and may be customized to provide shortcuts to other items as well.

paste

Pasting an **object** places an object that has been stored on the **Clipboard** at a desired location within a **document.**

presentation

A presentation is the completed PowerPoint product. It is a collection of all the **slides** put together in an organized informative manner.

primary key

In Access, the primary key is a distinctive **field** of a **table** that assures that each **record** is unique.

query

A query is a question you ask of an Access **database** to provide information on the data contained in the database.

record

A record is the total collection of data on one item or individual within a **table.**

report

In Access, a report is a presentation of data arranged to provide certain information.

row

In Excel, a row is an element of a **worksheet** that runs horizontally through the width of the worksheet. Rows are identified by numbers.

selecting text

Selecting text identifies the text on which you want to perform some procedure like adding text effects or removing it. The basic selection technique is to place your insertion point to the left of the text you want to select. Then press and hold the left mouse button and drag through the text until all the characters have been highlighted.

slide

Each screen in a PowerPoint **presentation** is called a slide; it is the essential element of the presentation.

speech engine

The speech engine is the software that makes the Speech Recognition feature possible.

Speech Recognition

Speech Recognition is the feature that allows you to speak into a computer microphone and then have Word translate your spoken word into the written word.

Standard toolbar

The Standard toolbar contains buttons most used in the operation of an application.

table

A table is a collection of data on one topic, for example, Customer's Orders. There may be many tables in a **database.**

template

A template is a special document with usage-specific formatting.

Thesaurus

In Word, the Thesaurus provides synonyms and antonyms of words.

transition

A transition is a type of **animation** that specifically governs the way one **slide** changes into the next.

value

Values, in Excel, are numbers you want to add, subtract, multiply, divide, or otherwise manipulate in **formulas.**

wizard

A wizard is an easy-to-use mini program built into an Office program that automatically performs a specific procedure for you.

WordArt

WordArt is a mini program that allows you to create artistic shapes with text.

workbook

In Excel, a workbook is a file containing **worksheets.** A new workbook contains three worksheets, by default, although it can easily be customized to add or remove worksheets.

worksheet

A worksheet is, in effect, one page of **data** within a **workbook.** A worksheet is very large, containing 256 **columns** and 65,536 **rows.**

Index

C

Calendar, Outlook
  adding appointments, 64–65
  appointments overview, 63
  configuring, 59–63
  Daily view, 60
  Month view, 62–63
  overview, 59
  setting print options, 46
  Week view, 61–62
  Work Week view, 60–61
cell references, worksheet
  copying, 119–20
  in modified cells, 113
  overview, 103–4
  relative vs. absolute, 119–20
cells, worksheet
  adding, 115–16
  aligning contents, 109, 110
  copying contents, 117–20
  deleting, 116
  formatting contents, 109–15
  glossary definition, 206
  inserting, 115–16
  merging, 110
  moving contents, 121
  naming, 116
  overview, 98
  rotating contents, 110
  wrapping text, 110
centered Word text, 87, 88
centered worksheet labels, 109, 110
chart area, 124
chart objects, 128, 129–30
charts, Excel
  adding text to, 127–28
  creating using Chart Wizard, 29, 125–30
  customizing, 132
  data comparisons, 130–31
  formatting, 132
  overview, 121–24
  types of, 126, 130–31

charts, PowerPoint, 157–60
chart sheets, 128, 129
chart titles, 127
Chart Wizard, Excel, 29, 125–30
checking spelling and grammar in Word, 93–95
clip art
  adding to PowerPoint presentations, 146–48
  glossary definition, 206
  inserting from files, 148–50
  inserting from Media Gallery, 146–47
Clipboard
  copying objects, 19, 20
  cutting objects, 19, 20
  in Excel, 117
  glossary definition, 206
  pasting objects, 19, 20–21
  shortcut for opening, 19
  terminology, 19
Clipboard pane, 19, 20–21
Clipboard toolbar, 117
closing files, 34–35
colors
  for AutoShape graphics, 152–53
  for Excel charts, 132
  tips for presentations, 169
columns, worksheet. See also fields, database
  adding, 115–16
  changing width, 112, 113
  deleting, 116
  glossary definition, 206
  hiding/showing, 113
  inserting, 115–16
  overview, 98
configuring Outlook Calendar, 59–63
Contacts list, Outlook
  adding names to automatically, 70
  adding names to manually, 70–71
  locating names, 71
  overview, 68–69
  setting print options, 46
  starting e-mail messages from, 71–72

E

editing Word documents
  formatting text, 85–92
  overview, 78
  removing text, 79
  replacing text, 79
  selecting text, 79–80
  using AutoCorrect, 81–83
  using AutoText, 84–85
  using Undo and Redo features, 80
e-mail
  adding names to Contacts list, 70
  attaching files to messages, 53–54
  creating messages, 50–54
  deleting messages, 56–57
  forwarding messages, 56
  generating messages from Contacts list, 71–72
  glossary definition, 207
  maintaining files, 56–59
  moving messages to folders, 57
  overview, 50
  receiving messages, 54–55
  replying to messages, 55–56
  searching for messages, 59
  sending messages, 53
  sorting Inbox messages, 58
embedded objects
  defined, 200
  in destination documents, 203, 204
  vs. linked objects, 199–200
  updating objects, 204
entering
  database data, 177–78
  Word document text, 75–78
  worksheet data, 100–108
errors, in worksheet formulas, 104–5
Excel. *See* Microsoft Excel
exporting Access tables to Excel, 192–93

F

Favorites toolbar, 18, 19
fields, database
  defined, 172
  in forms, 179
  glossary definition, 207
  in queries, 183
  removing, 175
  renaming, 175, 176
  in reports, 188
  in tables, 175–76
files. *See also* databases; documents, Word; presentations; workbooks
  closing, 34–35
  creating from File menu, 25–29
  creating from Standard toolbar, 24–25
  e-mail messages, 56–59
  existing, opening, 35–38
  naming, 30, 31
  new, 23–29
  opening, 35–40
  printing, 40–41
  recently used, 36–38
  recovering, 32–33
  saving, 29–31
filling worksheet cells, 121
folders
  adding to shortcut bar, 16
  displaying contents in Windows Explorer, 40
  moving e-mail messages to, 57
fonts
  applying effects, 87, 111–12
  boldface, 87, 111
  changing in Word documents, 86
  changing in worksheets, 111–12
  changing size in Word documents, 86–87
  changing size in worksheets, 112
  for chart text, 132
  italic, 87, 111
  underlining, 87, 111, 112
Format Cells dialog box, Excel, 110–11

formatting
  Excel charts, 132
  Word documents, 85–92
  worksheets, 109–15
Formatting toolbar, 10, 11, 20, 208
forms, database
  creating, 178–81
  defined, 172
  entering data, 178
  glossary definition, 207
  layouts for, 180
  naming, 181
  styles for, 180
formula bar, worksheets, 99, 208
formulas, worksheet
  cell references in, 103–4
  copying, 119–20
  entering, 101–3
  errors in, 104–5
  glossary definition, 208
  modifying, 113
  moving, 120
  overview, 102–3
  recalculating, 104
Form Wizard, Access, 178–81
forwarding e-mail messages, 56
functions, worksheet, 105–8, 208

 G

grammar checking, Word, 93–95
graphics, presentation
  adding to slides, 146–50
  AutoShapes, 150–53
  changing level, 148, 149
  clip art, 146–50
  moving, 147, 149
  resizing, 147, 149
  tips for presentations, 170

 H

Help system. *See also* Office Assistant
  accessing Web, 9
  overview, 4–5
  printing topics, 9
  using Answer Wizard, 7
  using Help Contents, 5–6
  using Help Index, 8

 I

importing
  Excel worksheet data into Access, 193–97
  Word outlines into PowerPoint, 143
Inbox
  illustrated, 48
  moving e-mail messages to folders, 57
  receiving e-mail messages, 54–55
  setting print options, 45
  sorting e-mail messages, 58
Insert Clip Art pane, 146–47
Insert dialog box, Excel, 115–16
Insert Function dialog box, Excel, 106–8
Insert Picture dialog box, PowerPoint, 148–49
italics
  in Word documents, 87
  in worksheets, 111

 J

justified Word text, 87, 88

 K

keyboard shortcuts
  for opening Clipboard, 19
  for opening Windows Explorer, 39

Slide Sorter view, PowerPoint, 136–37
sorting e-mail messages, 58
source applications, 200, 204
source data, 200, 201, 202
source documents, 200, 201, 203
speech engines, 78, 210
speech recognition
    establishing microphone settings, 77–78
    glossary definition, 210
    installing software, 77
    overview, 76
    training speech engine, 78
spell checking, Word, 93–95
Standard toolbar, 9, 11, 24–25, 210
Start menu
    Documents list, 38–39
    opening documents from, 38–39
SUM function, 105, 106
system clock, 63

T

tables, database
    creating, 174–78
    defined, 172
    entering data, 177–78
    exporting from Access to Excel, 192–93
    fields for, 175–76
    glossary definition, 210
    naming, 176
    setting primary key, 176
Table Wizard, Access, 174–77
target diagrams, 155–57
tasks, Outlook
    adding to task list, 72–74
    deleting from list when completed, 74
    maintaining list, 74
    overview, 72
    setting print options, 46
templates
    creating new documents from, 27–29
    glossary definition, 211
    vs. wizards, 29

text
    adding to Excel charts, 127–28
    aligning in Word documents, 87–88
    boldface, 87, 111
    editing in Word documents, 78–81
    entering in Word documents, 75–78
    italic, 87, 111
    line spacing in Word documents, 89
    overtyping in Word, 76
    removing from Word documents, 79
    replacing in Word documents, 79
    selecting in Word documents, 79–80
    speaking to enter in Word, 76–78
    tips for presentations, 169
    typing to enter in Word, 75–76
    underlining, 87, 111, 112
Thesaurus, 95–96, 211
time, setting in Windows, 63
time-series chart comparisons, 131
timing slide shows, 167–68
Title Master, PowerPoint, 135, 160
title slides, presentation, 134, 141
toolbars. *See also* Office shortcut bar; Office toolbars
    Accessories toolbar, 18
    adding to Office shortcut bar, 18–19
    Desktop toolbar, 18
    Favorites toolbar, 18, 19
    Programs toolbar, 18
    Quick Shelf toolbar, 18
transitions, slide, 135, 163–64, 211
typeface, changing, 86

U

underlining text
    in Word documents, 87
    in worksheets, 111, 112
Undo feature, Word, 80
updating
    embedded objects, 204
    linked objects, 202–3

V

values, worksheet
  copying, 117–18
  formatting, 109–10, 111
  glossary definition, 211
  labels for, 100
  moving, 121
Venn diagrams, 155–57
views
  Outlook Calendar, 60–63
  PowerPoint, 135–37

W

Week Calendar view, 61–62
Windows Clipboard, 117
Windows Explorer
  displaying folder contents, 40
  keyboard shortcut for opening, 39
  opening documents from, 39–40
Windows key, 39
Windows Start menu
  Documents list, 38–39
  opening documents from, 38–39
wizards
  Answer Wizard, 7
  Chart Wizard, Excel, 29, 125–30
  Form Wizard, Access, 178–81
  glossary definition, 211
  Import Spreadsheet Wizard, Access, 193–97
  Letter Wizard, Word, 92
  Query Wizard, Access, 182–84
  Report Wizard, Access, 186–91
  role in Access, 172–73
  role in Word, 92
  Table Wizard, Access, 174–77
  vs. templates, 29
Word. *See* Microsoft Word
WordArt, 153–55, 211

workbooks
  glossary definition, 211
  navigating, 99
  new, 25, 26, 28–29, 97
  overview, 97–99
worksheets
  adding cells, columns, and rows, 115
  adding to workbooks, 116
  aligning cell contents, 109, 110
  boldface text, 111
  chart location options, 128–30
  copying cell contents, 117–20
  deleting cells, columns, and rows, 116
  entering data, 100–108
  formatting, 109–15
  formulas in, 101–5, 113
  glossary definition, 211
  italic text, 111
  moving cell contents, 121
  Name box, 99
  overview, 98
  recalculating, 104
  underlined text, 87, 111, 112
Work Week Calendar view, 60–61
wrapping text
  in Word documents, 76
  in worksheet cells, 110

The manuscript for this book was prepared and submitted to Redmond Technology Press in electronic form. Text files were prepared using Microsoft Word 2000. Pages were composed using PageMaker 6.5 for Windows, with text in Frutiger and Caslon. Composed files were delivered to the printer as electronic prepress files.

Interior Design

Stefan Knorr

Project Editor

Paula Thurman

Layout

Minh-Tam S. Le

Indexer

Julie Kawabata

ARE YOU AN EXECUTIVE USER OF THE INTERNET WHO NEEDS TO GET STARTED QUICKLY?

Written specifically for busy executives, managers, and other professionals, *Effective Executive's Guide to the Internet* provides a fast-paced, executive summary of the seven core skills you need to know to use the Internet at work, on the road, or at home:

Skill 1: Understanding the Environment. This skill gives you an overview of the Internet: what it is, how it works, and how it came to be.

Skill 2: Making Internet Connections. This skill provides step-by-step instructions for connecting your computer or network to the Internet.

Skill 3: Browsing the Web. This skill focuses on the Internet Explorer Web browser included with all the latest versions of Windows. We explain how a Web browser works and how to customize Internet Explorer.

Skill 4: Communicating with Electronic Mail. In this skill, we describe how to use Outlook Express, the mail and news reader included with Windows.

Skill 5: Using Search Services. This skill describes in detail how search services work and how you can best use them. A special topic at the end of this skill gives you some ways to get started gathering business information.

Skill 6: Understanding Other Internet Services. In this skill, we look at FTP, Telnet, Mailing lists, and using your computer as a fax machine and telephone.

Skill 7: Publishing on the Web. Learn how Web pages work, how to develop a Web strategy, how to set up your domain and your server, how to collect and create digital content, and how to create your Web pages.

ABOUT THE AUTHORS:

Pat Coleman writes about intranets, the Internet, and Microsoft Windows 2000. Formerly the editorial director of Microsoft Press, Coleman is also the co-author of the best-selling *Effective Executive's Guide to Project 2000* and *Effective Executive's Guide to Windows 2000,* both published by Redmond Technology Press.

Stephen L. Nelson: With more than 3 million books sold in English, Nelson is arguably the best-selling author writing about using computers in business. Formerly a senior consultant with Arthur Andersen & Co., he is also the co-author of *Effective Executive's Guide to Project 2000* and *Effective Executive's Guide to PowerPoint 2000.*

288 pages, paperback, $24.95   Available at bookstores everywhere and at all online bookstores.
ISBN 0-9672981-7-2

ARE YOU AN EXECUTIVE USER OF WINDOWS 2000 PROFESSIONAL?

Written specifically for busy executives, managers, and other professionals, *Effective Executive's Guide to Windows 2000* provides a fast-paced, filtered executive summary of the seven core skills you need to know to use Microsoft Windows 2000 Professional at work, on the road, or even at home:

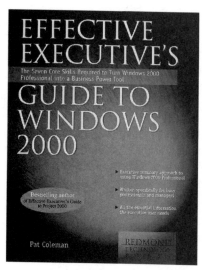

Skill 1: Understanding the Desktop. This skill explains logging on, using the Start menu, using the Taskbar, working with the desktop icons, and creating shortcuts.

Skill 2: Managing Files and Folders. This skill explains the Windows 2000 Professional file systems, including how to organize and protect your documents.

Skill 3: Printing. This skill shows you how to install and manage a local printer, how to print documents, how to customize the printing process, and how to install and use fonts.

Skill 4: Working on a Network. This skill gives you step-by-step instructions for setting up a small network, installing a network printer, setting up users and groups, and installing network applications.

Skill 5: Customizing Windows 2000 Professional. This skill suggests ways to customize everything from the display to the hardware.

Skill 6: Using the Internet. This skill tells you how to connect to the Internet and how to use Internet Explorer and Outlook Express.

Skill 7: Preventive Maintenance and Troubleshooting. This skill gives you guidelines for protecting the health of your computer, maintaining the system, and troubleshooting when a problem arises.

In addition, *Effective Executive's Guide to Windows 2000* also includes two appendixes that review the Windows 2000 Professional Accessories (including Address Book, NetMeeting, Notepad, WordPad, Fax Service, and Calculator) and explain how to use Windows 2000 Professional on a portable computer.

ABOUT THE AUTHOR:

Pat Coleman is a technical editor and author who writes about intranets, the Internet, and Microsoft Windows 2000. Coleman is also the co-author of the best-selling *Effective Executive's Guide to Project 2000* and *Effective Executive's Guide to the Internet,* both published by Redmond Technology Press.

304 pages, paperback, $24.95
ISBN: 0-9672981-8-0

Available at bookstores everywhere and at all online bookstores

Need a fast overview of PowerPoint 2002 so you can get back to your business or job?

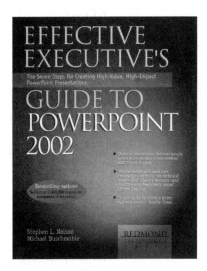

Written specifically for busy executives, managers, and other professionals, *Effective Executive's Guide to PowerPoint 2002* walks you through the seven steps of creating high-value, high-impact presentations:

> **Step 1: Learn the Logic.** Start here with an overview of what PowerPoint is and how it helps you make better presentations.
>
> **Step 2: Outline Your Content.** Create a textual list, or *outline,* of the messages and points you want to share.
>
> **Step 3: Add Objects.** Use tables, charts, and pictures to augment the information in your outline.
>
> **Step 4: Design Your Look.** Move past the substance of your presentation and address its appearance and "look" to create a professional presentation.
>
> **Step 5: Add Special Effects.** Use transitions, animation, sound, and video to enhance your presentation's impact.
>
> **Step 6: Prepare Your Presentation.** Prepare by creating speaker's notes, rehearsing, producing any handouts, and tailoring your presentation's slides for the presentation method.
>
> **Step 7: Deliver Your Presentation.** Deliver a successful, memorable presentation to your audience by comfortably using the appropriate PowerPoint tools.

Appendixes then suggest how to use Microsoft Graph and WordArt more effectively and explain how to customize PowerPoint. More than just a book about PowerPoint, *Effective Executive's Guide to PowerPoint 2002* explains how to make effective, compelling presentations that audiences understand and remember.

ABOUT THE AUTHORS

With more than 3 million books sold in English, **Stephen L. Nelson** is arguably the best-selling author writing about using computers in business. Formerly a senior consultant with Arthur Andersen & Co., he is also the co-author of *MBA's Guide to the Internet* (Redmond Technology Press, 2000).

The President of APPLAUSE! Associates, **Michael Buschmohle** has more than 40 years' experience delivering presentations to Fortune 500 companies and government agencies. He coaches CEOs, executives of high-tech firms, attorneys, U.S. mayors, and government officials on presentation and media skills. His clients have appeared on *Oprah, Good Morning America,* and the *Today* show.

256 pages, paperback, $24.95   Available at bookstores everywhere and at all online bookstores
ISBN: 1-931150-00-1

DO YOU NEED TO SET UP A WEB SITE FOR YOUR BUSINESS OR ORGANIZATION?

Written specifically for new Webmasters who need to set up a Web site for a business, a nonprofit organization, or a government agency, *New Webmaster's Guide to FrontPage 2002* walks you through the eight steps of designing, building, and managing a Web site using Microsoft FrontPage:

Step 1: Determine Your Web Site's Goals. Review common Web site goals and then identify goals that are appropriate for your site.

Step 2: Lay Your Foundation. Prepare the foundation of your Web site by getting a domain name and locating a company to host your site.

Step 3: Collect and Organize Your Content. Collect existing content or develop new content—then create a central warehouse to store and organize this material.

Step 4: Create Your Web Site. Set up your Web site and learn how to manage Web site files.

Step 5: Create Your Pages. Work with text, images, and hyperlinks to create and edit individual Web pages.

Step 6: Polish Your Pages. Create tables and advanced layouts to make your Web pages more consistent and effective—and then ensure that your Web pages properly appear in popular Web browsers.

Step 7: Add Interactivity to Your Web Site. Enhance your Web site by adding interactive features.

Step 8: Deploy Your Web Site. Test and publish your Web site and then draw attention to it by submitting your site to search engines, sharing links, using newsgroups and list servers, and generating offline publicity.

More than just a book about FrontPage, *New Webmaster's Guide to FrontPage 2002* explains how to create business and nonprofit organization Web sites that really work.

ABOUT THE AUTHORS

Jason Gerend, a Microsoft Certified Systems Engineer, has co-authored a series of acclaimed and best-selling computer books, including *New Webmaster's Guide to Dreamweaver 4* (Redmond Technology Press, 2001).

With more than 3 million books sold in English, **Stephen L. Nelson** is arguably the best-selling author writing about using computers in business. Formerly a senior consultant with Arthur Andersen & Co., he is also the co-author of *MBA's Guide to the Internet* (Redmond Technology Press, 2000).

304 pages, paperback, $24.95   Available at bookstores everywhere and at all online bookstores
ISBN: 1-931150-02-8